PINOCHET AND ME

PINOCHET AND ME

A CHILEAN ANTI-MEMOIR

MARC COOPER

VERSO

London • New York

First published by Verso 2001
© Marc Cooper 2001
Paperback first published by Verso 2002
© Marc Cooper 2002

3 5 7 9 10 8 6 5 4 2

The moral rights of the author have been asserted

Verso
UK: 6 Meard Street, London W1F 0EG
USA: 180 Varick Street, New York, NY 10014–4606

Verso is the imprint of New Left Books

ISBN 978-1-85984-360-4

British Library Cataloguing in Publication Data
A catalogue record for this book is available from the British Library

Library of Congress Cataloging-in-Publication Data
Cooper, Marc.
Pinochet and me : a Chilean anti-memoir / Marc Cooper.
p. cm.

1. Cooper, Marc. 2. Chile–History–1970-1973.
3. Chile–History–Coup d'état, 1973. 4. Chile–History–1973-1988.
5. Chile–History–1988– 6. Pinochet Ugarte, Augusto. I. Title

F3100.C64C64 2001
983.06′5–dc21   00-054983

Typeset by M Rules
Printed by Biddles Ltd, Guildford and King's Lynn

This book is dedicated to my two favorite Chileans, Patricia Vargas and Natasha Vargas-Cooper, to my departed *compañero* Roberto Naduris, and to the memory of my teacher, Salvador Allende.

CONTENTS

PREFACE: HOMAGE TO SANTIAGO

I first arrived in Chile in mid-1971, a half-year after the inauguration of the world's first freely elected Marxist head of state,
President Salvador Allende. I went to Chile originally as a
twenty-year-old Sixties radical. And I landed in Santiago,
frankly, as a sort of "social tourist" – an interested observer with
a couple of hundred dollars in my pocket and a head full of theories about social change.

By the time I fled Chile eight days after the September 11
1973 military coup as a UN-protected refugee, I had become
very much a participant. I had spent the previous year as
Allende's translator and, for that, I had become fair game for a
military dictatorship that considered people like me a "foreign
cancer."

I married into a Chilean family and have returned to Chile
several times since the coup – most recently around New Year
2000. On some of those occasions I came on private visits, but
most often as a working journalist.

But those twenty-seven months I spent in Chile during the

Allende period will forever mark me. Perhaps two decades or more of complex history were compressed into just a couple of dozen months. It was a period lived intensely by millions of Chileans – even by the most isolated peasants in the bitter southern extreme of their country – as well as by anyone else who had the good fortune to find him or herself in that wonderful country at that momentous point in its history.

Indeed, for many more millions around the world, Chile briefly shined as a beacon of inspiration. It gave life to the notion that, perhaps, radical social change and resulting improvements in the lives of common people were possible through democratic, peaceful, and legal means rather than through the violent and often treacherous turns of armed revolution.

In that sense, Chile was to be the exception in revolutionary history. But in other ways often overlooked, Allende's Chile was engaged in much more of a classic revolutionary scenario than that passed through by Russia or even Cuba. In Chile, the ascension to power of Socialist Party leader Salvador Allende came not as a result of the dogged tenacity of an armed elite. It was rather the culmination of fifty years of massive electoral campaigning for a democratic socialism. Socialism was not some novel idea that had to be announced or decreed during a post-election rally. It was, rather, something that millions of Chileans had been demanding for decades.

Chile, however, was the exception in that democracy was expanded – not rolled back – after the seating of a Socialist administration.

But this *revolución a la chilena* had inherent vulnerabilities.

And they all issued from the same source: trying to destroy a system by using the system itself. The police in the streets were the same ones who only a few years earlier had cracked workers' heads as a matter of daily routine. The court system was the same one that sent the workers with cracked heads to jail on charges of resisting arrest. The public administration was the very same depthless bureaucracy of the previous century.

And then there were the armed forces. While publicly professing loyalty to strict constitutional neutrality, the Chilean army had regularly been used throughout its history as armed representatives of Chile's wealthy elite. How long would it stand idly by and serve as armed guarantors and guardians of a new socialist order?

The answer to that came dramatically in September 1973. With the Chilean economy squeezed by a Nixon administration "destabilization" plan, with discontent in the streets fueled in part by CIA subsidies, the Chilean military put a fiery end to Allende's hopes for a peaceful transition to socialism. Led by General Augusto Pinochet, the armed forces bombarded the presidential palace I worked in, occupied every major city and town in the country and imposed what would become a seventeen-year-long night of dictatorship, death and terror.

Thousands of Chileans would perish under Pinochet. More than 1,100 would "disappear." Many thousands more would suffer imprisonment, torture, or exile. A century-worth of Chile's accumulated democratic and social advances would be bloodily dismantled overnight, and a new, radical capitalist order, presaging a wave of globalization, was built in its stead.

The long shadow cast over Chile by Pinochet would not only eclipse the brief Allende period but would persist for three decades or more. Even today, ten years after Pinochet relinquished power, after spending more than 500 days in British custody, being returned home and now sitting bottled up in the re-invigorated Chilean judicial system, he remains the single most important political presence in Chile.

This book is not a history text, nor a simple chronology covering the Allende and Pinochet periods. There are many and much better books available on contemporary Chilean history. This book is instead a personal journal. Part reporter's notebook, part diary, it consists of my reflections and observations written from inside Chile at several crucial junctures: in the last days of Allende, the week of the military coup, the tenth and twenty-fifth anniversaries of the dictatorship, and Chile, today, after Pinochet's arrest. The different sections of the book were written primarily during the dates indicated at the top of each chapter. In that sense, the different entries were produced contemporaneously with the events and reflections described. I have gone back over those writings and edited and pruned and compressed and expanded when necessary for explanation and context. But there has been no ideological or historical "re-writing." The inconsistencies in tone and perspective, therefore, are intentional. They embody the natural and bumpy road to maturation and insight that come with age and experience.

I call this an anti-memoir deliberately. A memoir attempts to re-assemble parts of a forgotten or fading past. But in Chile, the past has been systematically denied and more often brutally repressed. Collective memory in Chile has been erased as if the internal magnets of historical retention that reside in any national body politic had been given a massive jolt of electro-shock.

So my task is not nostalgic. In Chile the past has not been forgotten. In Chile the past has never been recognized. And without a sense of the past, a society has no future. This anti-memoir is a humble attempt to construct both.

Woodland Hills, California
September 2000

PRELUDE: "MY NAME IS PINOCHET"

NOVEMBER–DECEMBER 1971

On the day Fidel Castro was to arrive in Santiago, the sun, storming through my window, jarred me from sleep about ten minutes before Omar and Gunther came to pull me out of bed.

Omar had already made some *café con leche* by the time I was dressed and my kitchen had taken on the look of some sort of war room. My two Venezuelan friends were hunched and poring over a half-dozen newspapers all screaming with headlines about the imminent arrival of Cuba's *lider maximo*.

Castro was due to arrive at 5pm and then drive in a motorcade with President Allende the dozen miles into downtown Santiago. The three pro-government newspapers folded a special commemorative poster into their special editions: a three-foot-high rendition of Castro, his arm raised high, his finger pointing outward against a bright scarlet background.

I had been anticipating this event since my first day in Chile, four months previous. There was a tingle of history in the making. By renewing relations with Cuba and inviting its leader for an extended visit, Salvador Allende had dramatically broken the decade-long diplomatic and political embargo imposed by the United States. And Fidel's impending visit would have a direct personal impact on just about every breathing Chilean. He was either the embodiment of their most fervent revolutionary dreams or the personification of their darkest political nightmares. Omar and Gunther fell resoundingly into the first category. Both exiled Venezuelan guerrilla fighters, they viewed Fidel Castro as the undisputed authority on, well, just about everything.

As we headed into the streets that morning, Omar cracked a joke, saying he felt sorry for these Chileans. "They are, you know, very boring," he said with the sing-song lilt of Venezuelan Spanish. "They are the Englishmen of Latin America." These quiet Chileans who drank tea every afternoon, who addressed each other as "Madam" and "Gentleman," these Chileans who lived in such a non-tropical country that there was snow in the mountains, what – Omar asked – could these gentle Chileans possible make of all the throbbing, searing, stirring Caribbean passion that came with Fidel and the Cubans?

We all knew the answer. The stiff Chilean style was distant from the freewheeling Cuban spirit. But Chile now shared a certain destiny with Cuba. Both countries, each of them small, underdeveloped, and subject to much greater global powers, and consequently up against formidable odds, were – albeit by different means – striving to conduct radical transformations.

Ten blocks of Moneda Street separated my house from La Moneda – the presidential palace in which I would start working a year later. That stretch looked more or less the same as on any other day. It comprised a row of century-worn mini-mansions, gray, grimy, and crumbling. As recently as fifty years ago they housed the social elites of Chile – the Mattes, the Larraíns, and the Edwards. But slowly they were transmuted into decaying apartments and tenements teeming with the less elegant-sounding Gonzalezes, Rojas, and Contreras.

Once these buildings had descended into more common *barrios*, municipal governments lost interest in upkeep. Street lights were burned out, sewers plugged, the streets pot-holed, and the phone trunk lines in such disrepair that the waiting list for a new connection stretched toward a horizon of six to eight years.

Where an old landowners' club used to hold its weekly receptions, there now stood the district headquarters of the Chilean Socialist Party – its doorway festooned with a red flag and a portrait of Che Guevara superimposed on a map of Chile. And, that day, augmented with a flak of Fidel posters.

The colonial design of these dying buildings was rich in balconies, which displayed the only color on the street. A few were painted in blazing pink or yellow pastels, but nearly every one had a well-kept clover garden. From the upper-story windows, framed in wooden curlicues, splotches of political campaign posters left over from the 1970 presidential race could still be deciphered despite the tattering of wind and bleaching of the sun.

Most were a simple blue and gray portrait of Allende, his name spelled out on top of and underneath the slogan – "Venceremos!" – "We Will Win!" Here and there were occasional portraits of the grandfatherly Jorge Alessandri – the defeated conservative candidate of the oligarchs.

3

But now the street had been plastered with hundreds of new posters. It was like walking through a political rose garden in full bloom. Youth brigades of the Socialist and Communist Parties – the two major pillars of the Allende government – had spent the night covering up any blank wall in sight. And where blank space was scarce, they merely painted and pasted over the previous week's endeavors. The Communists had posted a long-reaching row of identical scarlet posters simply saying: "The Chilean Communist Party Greets Comrade Fidel."

The Socialists issued forth with a four-by-four black poster with an inflamed Latin America in the middle reading "The Socialists, Today Like Yesterday, With Fidel." All knew that this was a not-too-subtle snipe at the Communists who had originally failed to support Castro, writing him off as an "anarchist adventurer." The hard left MIR, the Movement of the Revolutionary Left, bitterly opposed to the timid policies of the Communists, and on the left fringe of the Socialists, had their own poster for the day – one pointedly featuring a photo of Fidel and friends holding rifles high into the air.

As the three of us crossed San Martín Street on our way to La Moneda Palace, we stopped for a time in front of the ramshackle headquarters of the Socialist Party Central Committee. The bustle from inside flowed nervously into the streets in front of the squat pink building: banners were being readied, pickup trucks were being loaded with boxes of leaflets and flags – all part of the "mobilization" to greet Castro.

Parked across the street from the Socialist headquarters was a beaten-up Willy's Jeep converted into a sound truck. And after a few crackling tests a scratchy version of the Socialist Party hymn, a modified "Marseillaise," began to blare, much to the delight of the thousand or so people right before us. Such a large crowd, so early in the morning, at this one minor staging point, portended the enormous numbers who would turn out to see Fidel. When the hymn concluded, the loudspeakers carried live radio coverage detailing preparations around the city. As reports of mobilizations rolled in from one workplace after another – especially from the large factories recently nationalized by Allende or simply seized by groups of workers – the crowd in the street would whistle and applaud.

Standing on the back of a pickup truck with me, my friend Gunther was starting to feel uneasy. He was wearing the bright scarlet shirt of the Communist Youth though he wasn't a member or even a sympathizer. He had bought the shirt some weeks earlier at a street rally merely because it was a bargain. But now, in this sea of Socialists – many in their own party-issue olive drab shirts – Gunther stuck out like a sore thumb. Socialists and Communists shared in the government. But rivalry between the two parties could at times be explosive.

Gunther's nervousness turned out to be well-founded. As I lifted my camera to take a picture of a group of Young Socialists pinning up a barrier, I noticed a young bearded man in an olive drab shirt starting to race toward me. "Comrade, for whom are you taking this picture?" he challenged.

I was furious. Not because I was being confronted but out of embarrassment for the boy himself. His behavior was uncalled for and beyond the bounds of acceptable behavior in Chile at that time. The Left never exerted any pressure on journalists. Allende's revolution was painfully democratic. And even if I had said, "Oh yes, I'm shooting for the CIA," the young man would have been powerless to do anything except perhaps politely ask me to leave.

About to answer my challenger, I was interrupted by an equally furious Gunther who told him that we were both Socialists ourselves and suggested that perhaps he had been watching too many American movies and had gotten the wrong impression about how a revolutionary should conduct himself.

The young man quickly apologized and gave us both a bear hug. Gunther, in turn, trying to take the edge off the encounter, invited him to join us as we proceeded toward La Moneda. We were planning to link up with some of Allende's press officials before heading off to the airport for Fidel's arrival.

He agreed to join us and began a lengthy monologue about himself. He was just nineteen years old; he had been an active Socialist since junior high school; his father was a director of the arcane Chilean Internal Revenue Service. And he said he lived a comfortable existence in the middle-class enclave of Providencia. Politically, he was uncomfortable and impatient of what he called Allende's "moderate, legalistic" road to socialism and he fervently hoped that Castro's visit would energize the more temperate Chilean revolution. His first name was Christian, he added, and he was a member of the Security Department of the Socialist Party – sinister-sounding but in reality akin to something like a monitor at an American anti-war march.

"I have French blood in me," Christian told us. "It's reflected in my family name. A family that has some importance in Chile," he said proudly.

I asked what his family name was.

He paused for a moment and then answered. "Well, it's not *that* famous. It's a name that Chileans might know. But not you foreigners. My name is Pinochet. Christian Pinochet."

At that moment, I had to admit, indeed, the name meant nothing to me.

We were headed towards La Moneda presidential palace. A 200-year-old grayish-brown fortress, it squatted over an entire city block. It had little aesthetic appeal, but was widely revered in Chile as the symbol of a century of democratic rule.

Allende had instituted an open-door policy at La Moneda. A couple of crisply uniformed *carabinero* police stood at the door but paid little attention to who was coming and going. When we arrived on the morning of Fidel's visit, the Plaza Constitución in front of the palace was vibrating with music, with swarms of people, and long lines of caravans. Thousands of demonstrators formed into circles, snake-danced, and sang the popular "La Batea," chanting and clapping, all waiting for President Allende to come out of his office and begin his journey to the airport to pick up his Cuban visitor. Across the plaza, the typesetters at *La Nación* newspaper had hung out a huge banner inviting Fidel to stay in Chile as long as he wanted. A delegation from the teachers' union, SUTE, was meeting in front of La Moneda, one of them strumming on a guitar while a dark-complexioned youth sang Allende's campaign song – "Venceremos" – through a battery-powered megaphone.

The *carabinero* guards at the Moneda entrance nodded us through into the expansive colonial courtyard upon which every palace office opened. The atmosphere inside was more subdued than in the street. We stood silently for about five minutes and watched an elite *carabinero* unit drill and march.

Of all the armed services, the *carabineros*, the uniformed national police, fascinated me most. They were a fiercely disciplined organization, the sharp cut of their olive-green uniforms reflecting the traditional German training they had received – right down to their goose-step marching.

The ironies were evident. This corps of *carabineros* under Allende was the same one that over the previous decade had been beefed up and honed to combat a rising tide of discontent from unions and students. They were the same cops who had fired on squatters in Puerto Montt under the previous government of Eduardo Frei. The same police who had jailed and beaten thousands of students throughout the Sixties – including Allende's own nephew, Andrés Pascal, leader of the MIR.

One of Allende's first acts in office had been to dismantle the *carabineros'* publically loathed riot squad which had been outfitted with small tanks, water cannons and even light artillery by previous administrations. But otherwise, the 30,000-strong Cuerpo de Carabineros had remained intact. Allende's Popular Unity government was relying on the "professional, constitutional, and apolitical character" of these corps. The same went for the armed forces in general.

There was also a calculation based on social class in this political gamble. The Left was banking on the modest economic background of most of the police – and of course – of the army's recruits. The carabineros were generally from workers' families and often lived in substandard housing in the squatters' villages – areas almost unanimously sympathetic to the Socialists and Communists.

Bottom line: The Left was asking for the loyalty of an armed institution that had gained its glories fighting left-wing workers' movements. This issue occupied my thoughts that morning as I watched the *carabineros* drill for Castro's arrival. But what was going through their heads? Their task that day was to risk their lives to protect the life of the Prime Minister of Latin America's only Communist government.

The *carabineros* were undoubtedly under strict orders to quell anything remotely like a disturbance that day. And a violent incident could not be ruled out. The Chilean Right was as passionate about Fidel's visit as was the Left. The right-wing tabloid, *La Tribuna*, was out with an edition that morning predicting that Castro would ride from the airport in a bullet-proof sealed car in order to "protect himself from the rage of Chilean democrats."

My buddy Gunther, staring transfixed at the drilling *carabineros*, wished out loud to me that no such incident would materialize. "I just don't trust these assholes," he said quietly, his eyes on the goose-stepping cops in front of us.

I had to agree. It was a bitter but unavoidable truth. For all of its warmth, color, fundamental justice, its commitment to democracy and its inspiration to others, there was nothing in the least certain or irreversible about what all called the "Chilean process" – Allende's peaceful revolution. Its very existence was due only to the continued goodwill of the *carabineros*, the Air Force, the Navy and the Chilean Army.

They were the only ones with guns.

We had come to the palace to see if we could hook up with some of our friends in the Presidential Press and Information Office and perhaps ride together out to the airport. But the crush and confusion of visiting foreign journalists had made it impossible even to talk to the people we had come to see. Omar suggested we go back out in the street and hop on one of the charter buses that had been caravanning outside La Moneda.

What we saw when we exited the Moneda was mind-boggling. In just the short half-hour we had been inside, the city center had exploded in carnival. It was no exaggeration to say that downtown Santiago had been occupied by workers, students, and their families. The Alameda, the central boulevard running in front of the palace and the main road to the airport, had been cleared of traffic. On the sidewalks, crowds ten and fifteen deep were staking out viewing positions while others were making the twelve-mile trek to the airport on foot.

Down the middle of the street, a parade of tractors carrying farm-workers, caterpillar trucks with hard-hatted workers, flat-bedded postal lorries loaded up with shabbily dressed but neatly combed laborers and their *señoras*.

In front of the Defense Ministry, diagonally opposite the Moneda, were a score of city buses that had been commandeered by groups of organized shanty-town dwellers. Each bus had been lathered with slogans (with water-based and removable paints!) and marked with the name of the shanty-town from which it originated: Campamento Lenin, Campamento La Bandera, Salvador Allende, Che Guevara, New Havana and eight or nine others.

On the streets, armed *carabineros* watched nervously, but stood idle, as brigades of MIR youth openly attacked wall after wall, covering up every available space with red and black posters. From loudspeakers mounted on the city light poles, the popular group Quilapayún sang the Spanish version of "We Shall Not Be Moved."

The Plaza Italia, which sits ten blocks east of the Moneda, is generally considered the UN official checkpoint between elite and popular Chile. Pass the Plaza and Alameda Boulevard's name is upgraded to Avenida Providencia. This is both a territorial and psychological barrier. Only on rare occasions would the street troops of the Left risk crossing into enemy territory.

But today, all bets were off. Lured by Fidel, the revolution edged up the Alameda, crossed boldly through Plaza Italia, entered the usually forbidden zone of the Señores and Patrones, and advanced wave after wave through the only tree-shaded streets in Santiago.

To the horror of the Providencia natives, this contagion was not spreading exclusively from the infected rear of society somewhere down in the workers' neighborhoods. No, it was also issuing from the very heart of their cultured enclave. Radicalized engineers, lawyers, writers, even some small business owners had come out of their political closets and on this morning had joined in the fervor, painting their

Citronetas or Peugot 404s with revolutionary slogans. Now they were riding around their neighbors' homes beeping wildly on their horns.

By 2pm, when the afternoon papers hit the stands, the Socialist-backed *Última Hora* was able to boast accurately that Santiago was firmly in the hands of the revolution, that the "streets belonged to the people," and that *momios* (the mummies, the reactionaries), after festering and threatening to sabotage Castro's visit, had "retreated to their living rooms after bolting the front door behind them and shuttering the windows."

Santiago's Pudahuel International airport sat in a field before us like a chunk of melting candy seized by a mammoth ant colony. Every patch and path around it, in it, on top of it, was crawling with people. The fields around it were jammed with every imaginable vehicle used to get people down here.

And the people out at the airport, the two, three, four hundred thousand of them, were, all clichés aside, definitely the *workers* of Chile, the class of people whom the residents of Provindencia and the upscale Las Condes neighborhoods disparagingly and regularly referred to as *rotos*. The literal translation is "the broken ones." The figurative translation is "nigger."

These *rotos*, this huge working mass of Chile, lived in a sort of social and economic apartheid. They dressed in suits of dull and often contrasting colors. They wore closed collars but could afford no ties. They spoke with a distinctive slum accent and more often than not opened their mouths to reveal huge gaps in their teeth.

The poorer among them, relegated to the shanty-towns that circled Santiago like a belt of misery, bore the marks of prolonged exposure to the elements. The running joke in Chile held that if the prime enemy on the Left was imperialism, close behind was bronchial pneumonia.

The children of these shanty-towns went to bed in shacks without windows and floors, the wind and rain whipping through the wooden slats. Malnutrition was a chronic problem among the bottom quarter of Chile's population. And too many children, and for that matter too many adults, could be seen wandering these shanty-towns with blank stares in their eyes – a symptom of severe mental retardation from generations of vitamin D shortage. It was no accident that the first point of Allende's forty-item electoral platform was a promise that the state would provide a free half-liter of milk to every Chilean child every day. In Chile of 1971 that was a revolutionary proposal.

But the one thing these *rotos* had in common was a fierce awareness of their social class – for no other reason than because it had been drilled into them by their *patrones*. Now, that identity, perhaps for decades turned shamefully inward, was finally being projected outward as a sort of political weapon.

What was captured that day at the airport, what made the entire Allende period stand out as different from the rest of the dreary past of the Chilean *roto*, was that the groveling deference to the rich and the handsome had been replaced by a revolutionary audacity. These people were proud of themselves. And it was heard in their song, their dance, their political debates, and casual conversation.

That afternoon of November 10 1971, as Fidel Castro's Ilyushin jet was on approach, Santiago finally belonged to those who for so long had been ignored and scorned. The airport was theirs. The city was theirs. The President of the Republic was theirs. And in just a few minutes, the one individual who, for better or worse, but certainly more than anyone else, symbolized a fight against poverty in Latin America, the man who cast a haunting specter over the wealth and power of their bosses, was about to land, to visit their country and to speak to *them*.

The explosive energy generated by Castro's arrival sustained itself through the entire twenty-three days of his visit. Fidel's processional through Chile moved from the capital to the northern deserts of Arica, to the copper mines of Chuquicamata, down to the coal pits of Concepción and into semi-arctic zone of Tierra del Fuego, and then back again to Santiago.

Wherever Castro went, usually accompanied by President Allende, a carnival, a rally, a day of speech-making and partying was bound to break out. The Chilean Right, meanwhile, retreated from the political stage, only to re-emerge on the next to last day of Castro's visit.

On the evening of December 1 1971 a terrorist bomb – the first of its kind in Chile's history – knocked out the electrical grid and plunged Santiago into hours of uncertain darkness. The follow-up punch was delivered the next afternoon. Some five thousand of Chile's wealthiest women, bedecked in jewels, some in party dresses, others accompanied by their maids and servants, and all banging loudly on pots and pans, staged what they called "The March of the Empty Pots." As they streamed from Providencia into downtown Santiago they cried out that they were hungry. They passed out leaflets with the absurd charge that "Marxists had cut off the food from the democratic areas of Chile."

What theater of the absurd! Here were the best-fed, best-clothed, fattest, and wealthiest people in Chile, many of whom controlled and owned the still private-sector food distribution system from top to bottom, claiming hunger.

This asinine spectacle would have passed unnoticed had it not been for the 200 or so helmeted youth shock brigades of the Christian Democratic and National Parties who accompanied the women. As soon as they hit downtown, the *brigadistas* erected barricades, smashed windows, fought with unionized construction workers, besieged the Communist Youth headquarters where they exchanged Molotov cocktails with the defenders inside, and attempted to burn down the multi-million-dollar UN building.

Carabinero detachments came into the streets and for the first time ever fought pitched battle with "rightists" through the night and into the next morning. More than 100 of the rowdies were arrested and over 150 people were injured.

The next morning, President Allende declared a state of emergency in the capital and the control of the police was transferred to the Army – specifically to the Commander of the Santiago garrison. As new disorder broke out, the Army

General ordered the police to use water cannons against the recalcitrant demonstrators.

By that afternoon, the left-wing tabloids were celebrating the swift and determined action of the General in charge. It was about time the other side tasted some steel, they averred. The General, the Santiago garrison commander, said the leftist press, should be decorated for his devotion to maintaining constitutional order.

The General's name was one I had never heard before – at least not in its entirety: Augusto Pinochet.

As soon as I read those words I taxied over to the Socialist Party Central Committee to look up my friend Christian Pinochet.

"Is this General a relative of yours?" I asked.

"He's an uncle. And he's an asshole," Christian answered sharply. He pulled the afternoon paper out from under my arm and read through the praises of Uncle Pinochet with mounting dismay.

"Don't believe a word of this shit," Christian said. "My uncle is no democrat. He's a fascist."

That evening on the national news General Pinochet made his first and only public statement about the outbreak of political violence. He warned all sides to cool their tempers and expressed the hope "that the police alone will be able to control the disorders. If they don't," said the General, "then the Army will have to come out into the streets, and do what they are trained to do: kill."

OMEN: ALLENDE'S DILEMMA

JULY 1973

Six months after Fidel Castro's departure I began work for
President Allende as a translator. After being asked by my
friends at the Presidential Press Office to work temporarily with
them during a six-week UN conference, I was invited to stay on,
putting Allende's writings and speeches into understandable
English. I accepted without hesitation and at the same time
applied to become a full member of Allende's Socialist Party. I
was twenty-two years old.

I could hardly call myself a personal confidant of the
President. We were separated by forty years in age and by a
couple of worlds' worth of political experience. But my close
contact with him only enhanced my admiration for the man,
politically and personally.

Salvador Allende was a hectically complex and contradic-
tory figure – romantic and rebel, revolutionary and
parliamentarian, Socialist and mason, physician and master
politician. He had few counterparts among politicians of the
twentieth century. Even his most bitter detractors had to admit

that few men were as politically canny. He was, indeed, the master of the felicitous maneuver. Yet at the same time he was desperately honest.

For thirty-five years he battled indefatigably for the interests of the *rotos* without ever being accused of betrayal or sell-out. More than any single individual Allende could claim credit for the myriad social legislation that had made Chile, even before his election, one of the most advanced democracies in the hemisphere.

When Allende spoke to crowds of 200,000 workers and their families, they would hang on his every syllable. In contrast to Castro's often demagogic posturing, Allende would speak more as a patient teacher, careful to review every detail.

Few politicians have been capable of such an eclectic repertoire of styles. When he appeared in public he would be greeted as Compañero Chicho (Comrade Curly, for his kinky hair). But this man of the people was also given to wearing debonaire turtleneck sweaters and tweed jackets, to dispatching *botas* of wine during his meals, to romancing the ladies. And, worryingly for his opponents, he had the knack of translating this personal charm into a gripping political charisma. Speeding through the crowded streets in his tiny Fiat 125, accompanied by a convoy of six identical cars crammed with rakish bodyguards, he would come to a halt in front of one of the hangouts of the super-rich, bound out of the car smiling, and enter the café to gulp down a creamy cappuccino while nodding pleasantly to the horrified right-wingers around him.

When incidents of this sort appeared in the next day's papers, he would be acclaimed by the lower ranks of the

Chilean population as a hero. His sense of humor was inexhaustible and infectious. A great fan of the movies, Allende would often go to see one of the latest Spaghetti Westerns with a couple of his bodyguards. One night while munching on popcorn he began to engage in spirited and loud dialogue with one of the characters on the screen who, having just shot down a band of desperadoes, was turning to leave them rotting in the sun. Allende bellowed out: "Hey! Hey! You could at least take their guns! If you don't need them, send them down here!"

Recognizing his voice, the audience jumped up and demanded he come to the front and say a few more words. Allende, always a populist, accepted the invitation. Part bourgeois *bon vivant* for sure, still more a sort of Marxist Musketeer.

But Allende also had a gravely sober side. In the 1960s and early '70s he was widely regarded as one of the continent's foremost radical leaders. The fiercely independent policy forged in the first weeks of his administration was quickly emulated throughout Latin America.

Allende nimbly straddled the ideological span of the modern Left. He was at once a dogged and tenacious defender of a human socialism, a friend and admirer of Che Guevara and a frequent visitor to Cuba. He was a founder of the Cuban-inspired Organization of Latin American Solidarity that served as a sort of coordinating committee for continental guerrilla war. And yet he believed with every bone of his body that the only path to socialism in Chile would be legal, parliamentary, and peaceful. He made no such prescription for other countries. But Allende was unmoveable in his conviction that Chile was different. As a young militant in the 1930s he had seen some brief, violent interruptions of his beloved Chilean democracy.

But absolutely nothing could have prepared Salvador Allende for the grueling dilemmas he faced during the third year of his presidency. By mid-1973, his Popular Unity government, his presidency, and Chile itself, stood poised at a daunting and ominous impasse.

Perhaps no single date better encapsulated Chile's predicament than July 26 1973.

On that day, Chile was no longer honeymooning with the dream of a peaceful revolutionary transition. Since Castro's visit, now a year and a half ago, Allende's government had scored some stunning successes. But so had the opposition. Class strife had blown apart the peaceful facade of Chilean politics. In the countryside a virtual ground war had erupted between increasingly well-organized landless and peasant movements who were dedicated to seizing massive farms and the oligarchs who owned the land. The orderly three-year plan formulated by Allende to nationalize the farms and compensate the *patrones* was sabotaged by a rightist-controlled Congress that blocked legal land reform. So farm workers simply took the revolution into their own hands.

At first Allende tried to dissuade the agrarian movement. But as hundreds and then thousands of farms were seized, Allende had no choice but to "legalize" the seizures after the fact. The agrarian sweep was encouraged by the Socialists and the MIR while the more moderate Communists openly fretted about the revolution going too far too fast.

In the months leading up to July 1973, some 50 per cent of Chilean agricultural land had been expropriated, either by the state or directly by farm workers. All farms larger than 175 acres had been taken. Now the peasant groups were planning phase two: seizure down to 80 acres.

The political atmosphere was just as hot in Chile's big cities, especially Santiago. On June 29 1973 a renegade tank battalion linked to an ultra-rightist cell staged what turned out to be a comic-opera coup attempt. Early that morning a few tanks rolled up to the Moneda and began lobbing shells and calling for a general uprising.

In those first uncertain moments, when the balance of power could have tipped in either direction, Allende, speaking through our Press Office network, called on the workers of Chile to take defensive measures by "occupying" all workplaces, farms, and factories. Within hours, the coup attempt melted away. But the factories were still in the hands of the workers. Embryonic workers' councils, which had previously been encouraged by the Socialists and bitterly denounced by the Communists, came all of a sudden into full blossom as veritable administrators and masters of the dark and dank industrial strips concentrated in four areas of the capital.

By July 26 1973 it was abundantly clear to all that the Councils had no intention of returning any of the major workplaces to their private owners. The Allende government was caught in a bind. It could not turn its back on its own popular base and use force to dislodge the workers. And yet,

Allende – and just about everyone else – had to know that this was all leading to a dangerous point of no return. Almost overnight, the worst nightmare of the Chilean elite had come to pass: in the space of a few hours they had been dispossessed of most of their productive wealth as the smoke-and-smog-smudged walls of the factory gates were draped with red flags and the surrounding cramped industrial neighborhoods turned into worker-run liberated zones.

Chilean socialism, measured by the economic and political power of the workers, grew more in one day – thanks to the botched coup attempt – than it had in the previous two years of parliamentary gradualism. The dialectic of peaceful change in Chile was clearly exhausting itself. The country had become a giant powder keg engulfed in a blaze of conflicting passions. The leading intellectual journal of the Left, *Punto Final,* editorialized: "For Chile, the cards are on the table. It will either be socialism or fascism – nothing in between."

The Chilean Right was hardly standing by idly. And in its anti-Allende efforts it was getting enormous help from the Nixon administration. Since the onset of the Cuban revolution, Chile, with its active and powerful electoral Left, had always been a central focus of US hemispheric policy. During the 1960s, for example, Chile was the largest per capita recipient of American Alliance for Progress funding. There had also been substantial covert CIA funding to Chile's Christian Democratic Party during the 1964 election, precisely in order to thwart one of Allende's earlier presidential challenges.

No surprise, then, that his eventual election in September 1970 set off alarm bells in Washington. In the Nixon White House, a special "Committee of 40" was established to monitor such events. And, indeed, a full two months before Allende's election, the administration's approach was established by Nixon foreign-policy guru Henry Kissinger, who told the Committee in reference to the predicted democratic electoral victory of Allende: "I don't see why we need to stand by and watch a country go Communist due to the irresponsibility of its own people."

While some on the Left – both in Chile and in the US – naively thought that Washington would take a more benign view of Allende's democratic ascension to power, Kissinger had a radically different notion. He thought that the example of a peacefully elected Socialist government coming to power was even more threatening to US geopolitical interests than the model of armed revolution. Large Socialist and Communist parties in France and Italy were gaining electoral momentum and Kissinger was plagued with nightmares of a Chileanized Western Europe weakening the anti-Soviet NATO alliance.

Efforts to stop Allende were already well under way immediately after his election and during the sixty-day window before his inauguration. The sinister euphemism of "destabilization" was introduced into the Cold War political lexicon. In cooperation with the White House, the International Telephone and Telegraph Company (IT&T) put up a million dollars for a secret campaign against Allende and in defense of the private Chilean phone system of which it was owner.

For its part, the CIA fashioned a two-track strategy. On the one hand, centrist and conservative Chilean politicians were offered CIA bribes to consider a parliamentary maneuver to block Allende's inauguration. (Elected in a three-way race with a 38 per cent plurality, Allende required a full majority vote of Congress to formally take office.) Simultaneously, the CIA developed a second, more violent, track in collaboration with a neo-fascist group. The plan was to kidnap the Commander-in-Chief of the armed forces and provoke a coup that would prevent Allende's inauguration.

Both approaches failed miserably. The bungled kidnapping of General René Schneider just two weeks before Allende's swearing-in ended with the General dying of gunshot wounds. The shock and revulsion, and the fear, that swept Chile were so great that whatever thoughts some politicians had entertained to deny Allende his due in exchange for American bribes were swept away by popular anger.

Allende was handed the presidential sash, but the US destablization program only escalated. At the close of one White House meeting on Chile, Nixon slammed his fist down on the table and barked orders to his CIA Director to make the Chilean economy "scream." American export–import credits to Chile were cut off. After Allende nationalized the Chilean holdings of the two American copper giants, Kennecot and Anaconda, with unanimous approval of the opposition-controlled Chilean Congress, the US economic embargo was drawn tighter. Relations further worsened when the Chilean government confiscated the IT&T-owned phone company and hotels.

The CIA covert program – several million dollars in total – also continued unabated. CIA funds flowed to anti-Allende political parties and their campaign organizations, to extreme right extra-parliamentary forces, to Chile's premier conservative daily, *El Mercurio*, and to various anti-Allende business groups like the powerful Truckers' Association. During the then-current transport industry work stoppage, the influx of CIA funding had been so great that, for the first time since Allende's election, the value of the US dollar plummeted: there were just too many greenbacks flooding the black market.

But during this entire CIA destabilization drive, the US government continued to maintain normal contacts and exchanges with the Chilean military, granting it millions in funding credits while the US strangled the rest of the civilian economy.

The CIA strategy, once Allende was elected, seemed not so much to conspire to stage a coup, but rather to lay the economic, social, and political groundwork to make such a coup likely.

The Chilean Right, always a formidable force, and now with its back to the wall, was delighted to receive such foreign encouragement. It had sensed that the corner had been turned and that it was now Allende who was on the defensive.

Chile is one of the few examples in history where a mass street movement of disaffected elites appeared as a significant political force.

The openly fascist group, Fatherland and Liberty, was swollen with new middle- and upper-class youth recruits and grew into a powerful and brutal militia. Sniper fire was directed at trade unionists in their houses, dynamite blasts took down

Communist and Socialist meeting places. Bombs were exploding in Santiago at the rate of three per night. Railroad track was being blown up and phone lines cut.

Allende's parliamentary opposition enthusiastically joined in the effort to remove the Popular Unity government by force. This openly confrontational strategy had been born earlier in the year after Allende had racked up a staggering electoral victory. In the March 1973 congressional elections, two years into the Socialist government, with inflation and food shortages rampant, street protests a daily occurrence, and the general chaos of rapid social change ever-present, Allende's coalition scored a 7 per cent increase over the vote in 1970 that had elected him to the presidency.

With Allende's popularity growing, the supposedly centrist Christian Democrats and rightist National Party threw in their lot with a strategy of military coup. On July 26 1973 the CIA-financed *El Mercurio* used its front page and seven-inch-high letters to reprint an open call to sedition by a leading Christian Democratic senator. He pleaded for the "armed forces of the Fatherland to clean out the workers from the illegally occupied factories and smash the Red Army being trained inside them."

Against this ominous backdrop, I joined with some 10,000 Chilean leftists who poured into the grimy, three-tiered, indoor Caupolicán Arena in downtown Santiago on the night of July 26. We had come ostensibly to celebrate one more anniversary of the Cuban Revolution. But that was merely a pretext. In the electric political atmosphere crackling around us, the rally became an occasion to assess our strength and test our focus.

Different organizations of trade unionists marched into the

cavernous auditorium, shouting out in unison the name of their occupied workplace and receiving wild ovations in return. Radical student groups followed behind them, some with steel helmets and carrying large bamboo sticks (a stark reminder of the military balance of forces should an armed confrontation be forced by the Right).

As the arena filled, the energy of the rally intensified. Clearly this was going to be one of the most combative leftist meetings ever. Passions were simmering. The radical MIR had a large following inside the rally and they heightened the atmosphere by stomping on the floor, clapping, and chanting their provocative slogan: "Political Consciousness! And Rifles!" Their militants combed the rally passing out leaflets defending the occupied factories and calling for all power to the Workers' Councils.

The Communists, meanwhile, upset by the extreme attitude of the MIRistas, returned their own verbal volleys. "Ultra-leftism Betrays Socialism!" they chanted back. This sort of verbal sparring was nothing new. Whilst there was a petty and divisive side to it, just as often it was merely light-hearted and competitive, a reflection both of the endemic sectarianism that plagues left-wing movements as well as the healthy plurality of opinion that laced Chilean socialism.

But beneath the cacophony of banter was a tangible sense of history in the making. Like the witnesses to the Russian Meeting of the Soviets at the Smolny Institute in October 1917, many of those present at the July 26 rally were aware that in a thousand different ways this event would survive the erosions and erasures of time.

Yes, the counter-revolution was poising for the kill. But Allende and the Chilean Left were going to fight back. The Caupolicán Arena looked to many of us that night like the first meeting of a Workers' Parliament. Hand-painted signs and banners proudly announced the presence of the Vicuña McKenna Workers' Council, the O'Higgins Council, the Cerillos Council, the Central Santiago Council. Fifteen-foot portraits of Allende and Che Guevara loomed above the stage.

The first speaker was Luis Figueroa, Minister of Labor. A former leader of the huge Chilean Central Labor Federation, Figueroa was an unimaginative and loyal adherent of the Communist Party. As he stood before the lectern, adjusting the microphones and fumbling through his notes, the entire crowd joined together in one roof-rattling voice, chanting: "*Allende! Allende! El pueblo te defiende!*" Allende! Allende! The People Will Defend You!

When the surge subsided, Figueroa began his speech. Within two minutes it felt as if someone had secretly thrown some invisible, sinister switch. The stirring blood-ecstasy that had inflated the auditorium popped. Like an invisible gas, the lethal tension that prevailed on the streets outside seeped into the arena and overcame the rally. Minister Figueroa, toeing his Communist Party line, began denouncing "adventuristic attitudes that could lead to civil war." This was a coded swipe at the Workers' Councils and those who supported them. Just as they had in the Spanish Civil War, the Communists were playing the role of the most conservative and anti-revolutionary force.

The Socialists, the MIR, and others loudly booed Figueroa

and tried to drown out his droning speech with new, more militant chants. The Communists escalated their slogan-shouting and soon Figueroa's voice was but a background hum behind a crescendo of shouting and jeering.

Here and there throughout the arena opposing groups faced off and exchanged blows and jabs with flag-poles and placards. The speech was cut short as the fighting spread. Attempts were made to calm things down, but when a leader of the Socialist Party took the podium after Figueroa, the Communists defiantly marched out of the stadium.

Amidst the soaring tempers and the deep divisions on the Left as to whether to go forward or retreat, the thousands at the rally that night ambled out of the arena with their spirits deflated, their hopes dimmed. The rally had collapsed amidst scenes that stood as a chilling portent. A Chilean photographer and fellow Socialist, Orlando Jofre, left with me and later that evening we huddled at our regular table in the bar at the Casa de La Luna Azul. Gulping his beer, he leaned back in his chair. "You know, we are so close – or rather we *were* so close. So close, but we aren't going to make it. It's all over, brother. It's all over."

It wasn't until the next morning that I learned that the tragedy of the collapsed rally was only the lesser, by far, of two that night. I got a message to come to the Moneda Palace immediately – our whole staff was being summoned. At 1am that morning, after returning from a diplomatic reception at the Cuban Embassy, President Allende's naval aide-de-camp, Arturo

Araya, a most gentle and endearing soul who was a favorite of everyone around Allende, had been assassinated in his home by the machine guns of a right-wing hit squad.

I was nauseated by the news and dressed quickly to go to the Palace. On my way, a second sickening jolt came in the form of a news report than an infantry division of the Chilean Air Force, acting on its own authority, had conducted a raid against one of the largest worker-occupied factories searching for "illegal weapons." The propaganda campaign of the Right had, it seemed, taken root in the armed forces. The uneasy three-year marriage between Allende's peaceful socialism and Chile's military now seemed as much a cadaver as Commander Araya's bullet-riddled body.

And in spite of the right-wing claims, the Chilean Left was essentially unarmed.

I got to the Moneda Palace and stood with several hundred others of the President's staff and cabinet waiting for Allende to arrive. He finally pulled up in the cortege that carried Araya's corpse. The President joined as one of the pall bearers carrying Araya into the palace where he would lie in state. As so often in times of crisis during the previous two years, I turned to President Allende for strength. His demeanor and careful oratory were always infused with a snappy resilience. But on the cloudy morning, as I scoured his face for some sign of strength and optimism, I instead found the depressed countenance of a deeply saddened and disappointed man. I turned to walk into my office. I was troubled. And, frankly, I was scared.

DELUGE:
CHRONICLE OF A DEATH POSTPONED

SEPTEMBER 1973

7am, Tuesday September 11

The fledgling Santiago sun and the transparent sky, the fresh spring chill in the air, and the blossoming jacaranda made that Chilean morning of September 11 1973 glorious. As I stood in the yard of my friend Melvin's suburban house and glanced at the lingering snowcaps on the Andes towering right behind me, as I sucked the fragrant, misty air into my lungs, I resolved I would, from that moment forward, make a sea change in my life. Quit smoking, cut back on drinking, get to bed before 3am and start rising earlier so as to enjoy more frequently these morning wonders.

I had gotten up early because my Chilean residency visa expired that day and I needed to renew it – an arduous process. For a year now I had been working as a translator to President Allende and, in this capacity, I was scheduled to travel with him the next week.

I knew that presidential translator status would afford me little advantage in navigating Chile's byzantine bureaucracy. Renewing my visa would still take the entire morning. And getting an Argentine visa so I could travel with Allende to Buenos Aires for the inauguration of the new Argentine president would take the rest of the day. An early start was imperative.

Taxis had become harder to come by as many of the cab companies had joined the work stoppage led by the Truckers' Association – a group floated with CIA dollars. Retail merchants, doctors, lawyers, almost everyone more elevated than manual workers and farmers had joined the stoppage. In daily entreaties, they pleaded openly with the armed forces to do away with the popularly elected Allende and restore Chile to Business-As-Usual.

Indeed, Chile had already pitched itself into a dizzying dance of chaos and blood. As Allende's reforms deepened, as he nationalized the American copper mines and telephone company, as large rural estates were handed over to their share-croppers, as wages soared and unions gained a voice in national affairs, as rents were lowered and taxes on the rich increased, the political Right and eventually the Centre jettisoned their attachment to the rule of law. Opposition groups fielded chain-swinging thugs against government marches. Oil pipelines were dynamited. Industrial production was sabotaged. The wealthy hoarded food and other consumer goods and then loudly protested the resulting shortages.

Just a week previous to this morning, on September 4, the Chilean Left held its last great public gathering to commemorate the third anniversary of Allende's election. While the

President stood granite-faced on a balcony from the early afternoon till late into the night, more than a half-million Chilean workers and their families marched before him, voicing the nearly unanimous chant: "We want guns! We want guns!" It was a horrible, wrenching moment, one permanently seared in my consciousness. Yes, guns. But what guns? From where? And how? My friends and I walked home that evening with a dark foreboding. The end was surely near.

In the seven days that followed, the Right drew the noose tighter. Commerce and transport ground to a halt. The night before September 11, the transport stoppage had waylaid me and my girlfriend at Melvin's house. We had gone out as a foursome, wound up snacking at Melvin's, and got stranded without a way back to my downtown apartment.

My only chance of transport that morning was with my friends at RadioTaxi 33. Militant revolutionaries, the drivers there had long ago seized the company from its conservative owners and had turned the place into the most efficient cab service in Santiago. And when the drivers weren't working their shifts, they'd volunteer as drivers and messengers for the most powerful workers' council in Santiago, the Cordon Vicuña McKenna.

After a forty-five-minute wait on the corner, I became concerned. I went back to the house to call the taxi company again but, inexplicably, the phone lines were now permanently busy. I walked back to the corner and eventually was able to flag down a passing cab.

The driver, pale and harrried, rolled down the window. "Can you take me downtown?" I asked.

"Downtown?"

"Yeah. To the immigration office," I answered.

With classic Chilean understatement and cool diplomacy the cabbie replied: "But, sir, there are problems downtown."

"Problems?"

"Yes, problems," he said refusing to be more specific. After all, these were highly polarized times. You never knew who you were talking to. One person's problem was another person's liberation. But a sinking feeling in my gut told me the worst was upon us.

Mustering my own diplomatic skills, I asked. "Problems, you say? Problems with men in uniform you mean?"

'Yes, sir, problems with men in uniform," the cabbie said. But now, the fear of the future already imprinted on him, he took what he probably knew would be his last foray into freedom for some time and added: "Yes, the fucking fascists are overthrowing the government."

7.55am, Tuesday September 11

Everyone else in the house was still asleep. I switched on the massive Grundig radio and waited impatiently for the vacuum tubes to warm up. As the audio came alive I turned the dial and confirmed the cabbie's report: virtually every station was playing the same military march.

I stopped the dial on Radio Corporación, the station of the Socialist Party. Allende was speaking, a nervous inflection in his voice. His words made material the nightmares that had haunted us for months: "This is the President of the Republic speaking from La Moneda Palace. Confirmed reports indicate that a sector of the Navy has isolated and occupied the port city of Valparaiso, which means an uprising against the government is under way . . . Under these circumstances, I call upon the workers of the country to occupy your workplaces . . . but I urge you to stay calm. At this moment, there have been no extraordinary troop movements in the capital . . . I am here defending the government that represents the will of the people . . ." Allende assured those listening that he would be back with any further information but that for the moment we should all remain in a state of alert.

On just about every other station on the dial a stern-voiced announcer suddenly materialized. By order of the military junta, he said, all radio stations were immediately to link up to the armed forces network or "they will be bombarded." The names of the four commanders making up the junta were then read: leading the National Police – the *carabineros* – was a general César Mendoza, a little-known name. For the Air Force there was Gustavo Leigh and for the Navy, Admiral José Merino. But the most important person on the list was Army General Augusto Pinochet. Pinochet, previously the Commander of the Santiago garrison, had two weeks earlier taken over as Commander-in-Chief, swearing his loyalty to the President he was now trying to overthrow.

Some more Prussian marches. And then another announcement. An ultimatum to President Allende. I sat chilled and shaking as I strained to scribble down the text of what a steely voice called Military Communiqué Number 2: "The Moneda

Palace must be evacuated before 11am otherwise it will be attacked by the Chilean Air Force. The workers must remain in their workplaces and homes as it strictly prohibited to leave them. If they disobey, they will also be attacked by air and ground forces."

I sat paralyzed. A few moments later the same dry baritone voice read out Communiqué Number 3. Again I noted it on a yellow pad. "The population is hereby warned not to let themselves be carried away by incitements to violence from either foreign or national activists. And let the foreign ones know that in this country we do not accept violent attitudes or any extreme positions. This should be remembered as means are adopted for their rapid deportation from the country. Any resistance will be met with the full rigor of military justice."

Yet another announcement proclaimed a curfew "until further notice." Anyone found on the streets "will be shot on sight." I had roused the others in the house. We sat dumbfounded in the chilly living room listening to Radio Magallanes, the Communist Party station, boldly resisting the order to broadcast the armed forces network. Over the air, workers were being urged to report to their factories and organize defense committees.

But this was an empty gesture. Those of us who worked in the Allende government knew the sad truth: that in spite of the right-wing chorus that Allende had formed a "parallel army," we had no such units. Allende had been scrupulous in his commitment to a constitutional, legal, and peaceful transition to socialism. The only guns in the country, he vowed, would remain in the hands of the armed forces. Yes, some Socialists and others had formed clandestine militias – but they were operationally risible.

This war was going to be a short, one-sided massacre. And the tragic irony was that those conservative and centrist political forces that for 150 years had defended a constitutional system as long as it served their interests were now rebelling against it. The last man left standing in defense of the "bourgeois" constitution would be the Marxist President, AK-47 in hand.

10am, Tuesday September 11

Miraculously, my first attempt to phone the office where I worked in the Moneda Palace went through. Over the sound of crackling gun fire, a secretary, Ximena, told me in tears that she and the others were about to flee the building. My next call was to the US Embassy – up on the fourteenth floor of an office building diagonally opposite the Moneda. I had had virtually no contact with the Embassy and had, in fact, made every effort to steer clear of it. Even my mail was routed to the Canadian Embassy – a government that had showed more sympathy to Allende.

But I phoned the US Embassy that morning hoping that some safety provisions were being made for resident Americans. I figured it was only a matter of hours before I would be swept up in the military dragnet.

The Embassy phone answered on the first ring. An accented English told me I was speaking with a Chilean employee – always more American than the Americans. When I asked if the Embassy had issued any special instructions, my respondent only laughed. "No special orders. Just stay off the streets." And then with another chuckle she added: "I'm looking out the window now with binoculars. Looks like Mr. Allende is finally going to get it." She hung up.

11am Tuesday September 11

The leftist Radio Corporación and Radio Portales are off the air. But Salvador Allende's metallic voice is coming live over Radio Magallanes. Via telephone, from inside the Moneda, with troops and tanks poised outside, with the Air Force Hawker-Hunter jets arming their rockets in readiness, Allende spoke:

> This is surely the last opportunity I will have to address you. The Air Force has bombed the towers of Radio Portales and Corporación. My words are not bitter but they are full of disillusionment. And they will serve as moral sanction for those who have betrayed their oath of loyalty: the soldiers of Chile, the branch commanders . . . Admiral Merino who has named himself Chief of the Navy . . . Mr. Mendoza, a slinking general who only yesterday swore his loyalty to the government, who has proclaimed himself head of the Police . . .
>
> In the face of these events I can only say this to the workers. I will not resign . . . With my life I will pay for defending the principles dear to our nation . . . History cannot be

stopped by repression or violence . . . Surely Radio Magallanes will be silenced and with it my voice. But that's of no importance. You will continue hearing me as I will always be by your side. At least you will remember me as a man of dignity, a man who was always loyal to you . . . You must know that, sooner rather than later, the grand avenues on which a free people walk will open and a better society will be at hand . . . These are my last words . . .

I sat stunned and devastated. I can only remember the four of us in that living room listening and sobbing for I don't know how long. The fear was palpable. To go onto the street was to risk arrest or execution. We had no access to any information except what the military broadcast over the radio. The phone lines were now dead.

Everything I had learned over the previous two years told me the Chilean Revolution had come to its end.

4pm, Tuesday September 11

A non-stop cascade of military communiqués: that the Moneda had been bombed, that the Allende government was no longer, that all political activity was banned, that a dawn-to-dusk curfew was in effect, that the citizenry should denounce all "suspicious foreigners." As that first evening under military rule enveloped us I felt as if I were already in prison.

I knew I was a prime target: Allende's translator, an activist in the radical wing of the Socialist Party and a foreigner to boot at a moment when *all* foreigners were *ipso facto* suspect. I thought of my own apartment and cringed, a downtown high rise located directly across the street – no more than twenty yards – from the new junta headquarters. Régis Debray, the French writer and radical who had spent time with Che Guevara in Bolivia, had lived in my building when Allende first came to power. Other units were rented to exiled guerrillas from Argentina and Uruguay. The building teemed with the international New Left. One room of my apartment was stocked with the cheap editions of political classics and classic fiction made available under Allende. On my studio desk were copies of the work I had translated for Allende. In my top drawer was my passport, a visa to Cuba where I was scheduled to visit with Allende, and to top it all off, a .22 revolver with a couple of boxes of ammunition. On the floor were two radio transceivers that I was repairing for my buddies at RadioTaxi 33. In short, once the troops broke into my apartment, as they undoubtedly would, a warrant would be issued for a twenty-two-year-old American named Marc Cooper.

Tuesday night to Thursday night, September 11–13

Those days were passed in the sort of blur produced by a state of deep shock. All that remains now is a kaleidoscope of images provided with a semblance of meaning by scraps of hurried, sometimes incoherent notes. I know I didn't sleep that first night. I imagined Allende riddled and bloodied on his office floor. I could see the Moneda reduced to rubble by rockets and fire. The following morning, an official communiqué announced that Allende had committed suicide.

The resumption of Chilean TV. A wavering, black-and-white image – now in the annals of history's infamy – of General Pinochet sitting ramrod straight in the presidential chair, his arms crossed across his chest, Ray-Ban Wayfarers hiding his dulled eyes, his accomplices in the junta standing beside him.

I thought of the poor neighborhoods and factories, now surrounded and invaded by vengeful troops. I wondered about my friends: about Vicente and an American named Vince; about Ximena, Jorge, Orlando; about the journalists, the co-workers. How many were already dead? How many would I ever see again? How long would it be before the troops came crashing through Melvin's door to take me away?

I thought of the celebrations no doubt taking place that night in the lush suburbs of Providencia and Las Condes. I listened to the radio and noted down the congratulatory notes pouring in to Pinochet from the Doctors' association, the Lawyers' Guild, the Chamber of Commerce, the Truckers – all the business sectors that had paved the way for the coup.

On Wednesday a statement from Supreme Court Chief Justice Enrique Urrutia affirming the court's "pleasure" with the military takeover. A terse military statement suspending habeas corpus and announcing a declared State of Siege. Military Communiqué Number 29 dated September 13: "On this date the government junta has decreed the following: The closure of the National Congress and the vacancy of all its parliamentary seats. Signed, the governing junta of the armed forces and *carabineros* of Chile."

I winced at what I knew would be the wave of bloodletting, homicide, and torture that was about to wash over Chile. I wondered how the hell I was going to get out alive.

I remember getting up at 4 in the morning and shaving off my beard. I remember opening my wallet and taking out my union card, my Socialist Party membership, my ID from the Moneda, and setting them ablaze. Those two days after the coup, Wednesday and Thursday, were marked by the sort of looming madness that I imagine accompanies solitary confinement. We had little food in the house. Melvin – a thirty-year-old Bronx-born American – had never told me why he was in Chile. I had always assumed he was ducking a drug possession charge coming out of the Sixties. A fervent Allende supporter, and a fervent capitalist, he made his living buying and selling on the black market.

The only food in the house was a freezer full of Eskimo pies, several sacks of onions, and a case of Pisco liquor. This odd diet, peppered with fear and haunted by uncertainty, drove me into a feverish, swirling retreat. I could barely talk to my Chilean girlfriend – now my wife – Patricia. I slept, I paced, ate ice cream, read Jim Thompson novels, cried, and waited either for the curfew to lift or the door to come crashing down. But mostly we sat and listened to the radio. List after list of the wanted: Allende's cabinet ministers, party activists, union leaders, prominent and not so prominent exiles had their names read over the air and were ordered to surrender at the Ministry of Defense. How they were supposed to even step out on the curfew-swept streets without getting shot was never explained. As every announcement began, I was sure my name would be next.

10am, Friday September 14

Melvin and his girlfriend have drunk themselves into a stupor.
As the radio announces that the curfew will for the first time be
lifted today for five hours, Patricia and I decide we must leave
Melvin's. She had to check on her family. I had to get my passport out of my apartment and figure a way to safety. Two weeks
before the coup my former roommate Carlos Luna, an exiled
Argentinean guerrilla fighter, showed up at my apartment with
a 9mm automatic. "The shit is coming," he said pulling the
pistol from his jacket. "When it does, I am getting into the
Swedish Embassy even if I have to shoot my way in." But I had
no such formidable weapon nor such courage. The military
had already announced that it had put rings of troops around
European embassies. I wondered where Carlos was. Was he
dead by now?

My impulse to flight was heightened when, during the break
in curfew, a client of Melvin's, a deli owner, came to the house
in his 3-cylinder Citroneta. Well-connected to the military, I
took his words at face value when he told me matter of factly,
"Cooper, you're fucked. Your apartment has been raided and
they're out looking for you," I asked him to drive me somewhere safe. He refused.

A numbing panic gripped me. For the next four hours I
could move, but I had nowhere to go. My apartment had been
trashed, I was told, my passport seized, my name was on a
wanted list, and the streets were full of soldiers and checkpoints. The phone started working again. In what must have
been the moment of greatest naivety in my adult life, I thought

again of the US Embassy. I had an image in my head from Rossellini's *Rome: Open City*. I could see the grainy black-and-white footage of Embassy staff cars rushing around the battle-littered streets, their white flags flapping.

I am embarrassed now, years later, to confess that I thought that, given the mounting bloodshed in Chile, the American Embassy on that day would be sending out rescue cars to pick up beleaguered stragglers like myself. I was under no illusions as to where the Embassy was at politically. The Nixon–Kissinger regime had made clear its intention to do away with Allende and it was now three days deep into implementing that goal. But I was deluded enough to think that, in order to avoid the uncomfortable spectacle of American citizens being killed by its new client military dictatorship, the US government might do something to protect us. In this I was entirely wrong.

As the curfew temporarily lifted that Friday I called the US Consulate. Explaining merely that I was an "American student," that I had done nothing wrong, but that the Chilean Police had raided my apartment and seized my passport, I told the Vice-Consul, Mrs. Tipton, I needed help. Even as I asked, my heart began to sink. Her husband was the Embassy's top "political officer," tied to the darkest aspects of US policy.

"Do you have a US driver's license?' Mrs. Tipton asked me. "Yes."

"Good," the Vice-Consul said. "Don't bother to come in today because we're about to close. But come in on Monday. Bring your license and ten dollars and we'll expedite you a new passport. Should take about a week, maybe ten days."

Stupefied, I argued with her. But to no avail. No special

instructions to US citizens were being offered. "Just stay away from shooting and obey the new authorities," she said. As far as the Embassy was concerned, my predicament was a simple case of a lost passport.

They certainly knew better. But the political calculation had already been made. It was more important to give political support to the new dictatorship than it was to undermine its credibility by suggesting that American citizens needed protection against it.

Noon, Friday September 14

Turned away by the Embassy, I was now desperate. I rummaged through my mental Rolodex and focused on a long shot. An American friend of mine, an *Allendista*, had told me some months before that a guy named Dennis Allred, who served as the US Embassy's Student Affairs Counselor, was a decent man, a closet Allende sympathizer who took secret delight in handing out US scholarships to the most radical of Chilean students. True or not it seemed like the only chance I had.

I phoned the Embassy back. No, I was told, Mr. Allred wasn't in. But, yes, being a fellow American, I could have his home phone number. "Dennis, you don't know me," I told him after he answered his phone. "But I'm an American and I'm in trouble. I need . . ."

"OK," he said, cutting me short. "I don't care about the details. If you need a place to stay you're welcome here. Come now. I'm at Merced 280."

I thanked him and hung up. Merced 280? That would put him right next door to the heavily guarded US Consulate. Could I get past the troops? Patricia and I hurriedly made a plan. She would catch a bus to her parents' home but first would swing by my apartment and check its condition. She would call me later at Allred's. I would walk the seven miles to Allred's house as I had no ID and buses were being boarded and checked by soldiers.

My clothes were filthy. Melvin, who is 6' 2", lent me a pair of pants. I am 5' 3". I tucked the bottom of the pants up and pinned them inside with safety pins. He gave me a fresh shirt and I rolled the sleeves up over my wrists. On top of this unlikely outfit I wore my black leather jacket. For three hours I trudged toward Allred's house, protected only by sunglasses, taking side streets and looking far ahead for any checkpoints.

By 4 o'clock I was on the perimeter of the US Consulate. Neighboring Forestal Park was literally an armed camp. Armored carriers bristled with machine guns and helmeted troops. In front of the Consulate, a few steps from Dennis Allred's apartment, a company of soldiers lounged on a tank. I could hear my heart beating in my ears. I had no idea what I would tell the soldiers if challenged. I walked straight ahead, my eyes fixed on the door of Allred's building, my pace steady. Like passing through a time warp, I floated into the building uninterrupted.

A big, red-headed Bostoner, Allred greeted me alone in his luxury apartment. I was so pent up I could hardly talk at first. And then I began to talk too much. "I don't need to hear the details of your story. You can stay here as long as you have to," he said. He then offered me a tumbler full of Old Grandad which I gulped down like water. The booze took the edge off, and I slumped back in the broad padded mahogany chair. I called Patricia at her parents' house. I was relieved to hear that my apartment had not been raided. She had got in, picked up my passport and a couple hundred dollars, and tossed my .22 and the two boxes of ammo down a garbage chute. She would come and visit me the next day when the curfew was again to be lifted for a short time.

Over a real meal that evening – salad and Kraft macaroni and cheese – Allred told me the news, good and bad. "This apartment theoretically has diplomatic immunity, theoretically Chilean security cannot enter," he said. "On the other hand, the morning of the coup, the US Embassy took my passport, locked it in a safe, sent me home, and told me they'd call me when I should come back to work. So I don't know how much protection we really have." I could only guess that the stories my friend had told me about Allred were true.

That night, on the convertible bed in his den, the saddest of Portuguese *fadas* I had fished out of Allred's record collection drowned the sounds of sporadic gun fire and the rumble of tanks outside my window. With a strong sleeping pill Denis gave me I slept soundly for the first time in almost 100 hours.

6pm, Sunday September 16

The word was apparently out on Allred's generosity. Over the weekend the apartment filled up with other hunted prey. A few had been beaten and bruised by troops who had broken down their doors. Others, like me, had nowhere to go. Still others were there because I had contacted them. Allred had taken the courageous step of abandoning his direct-dial diplomatic phone to us – a luxury in a country where long-distance calls even under optimum circumstances were difficult to make and where now so-called "press-calls" of the sort we were making had to be cleared by a military censor. With Allred's phone we skipped over those obstacles.

In Allred's study we set up a mini information clearing house. We called around the city to check on the safety of over-lapping networks of friends and co-workers. Once the information was compiled from a mongrel mix of sources – friends, friendly reporters, diplomats, health workers, UN func-tionaries – we were able to skirt Chilean censorship and pass the information directly on to family, media, and human rights groups in the US. Painstakingly, we cobbled together lists of those safe, those arrested, and those simply missing. But there was still no way out of Chile. The airports were closed, the embassies sealed. Any foreigner on the street was *ipso facto* a sus-pect. Who knew who was on the myriad wanted, arrest, and kill-on-sight lists? We already knew the US Embassy was useless.

A friend of mine, a Mexican reporter, called me from his Embassy. Would I be interested in getting on a list that the Mexican Embassy was putting together to be evacuated? "Absolutely," I answered. I gave him the names of three or four other desperate friends. He told me to sit tight and wait, that word of the flight out could come at any time. I had no choice but to comply.

A few friends who had come to see me at Allred's told tales of serious resistance, of a regrouping of Allende forces, of guns that were on their way, of former Army General Carlos Prats, forced from office a few weeks before the coup, who was now pulling together a People's Army. The rumors all sounded wonderful. And we knew they were all false. The Chilean armed forces, the CIA, Nixon, Kissinger, the Chilean business elite had won their victory early that first morning when the Army didn't divide and when Allende perished inside the Moneda. Now they were just mopping up the rest of us.

Noon, Monday September 17

Word had come that some Americans were missing. David Hathaway had been taken from his apartment. Frank Teruggi was unaccounted for. Sometime that day, our friend Charlie Horman would be seized.

During my time in Chile I had only limited contact with the American expatriate radical community. Some of them had come together in a group called Fuente de Información Norteamericana (FIN), which struggled to gain a voice as an alternative source of information on Chile to the mainstream media. I had no participation in that project but, for a short time shortly after I arrived in Santiago, I spent a string of Saturday mornings in a "study group" with Frank Teruggi and others. I soon tired of those meetings and what seemed to me at the time their uncritical attachment to the MIR. But I always thought fondly of the spry and witty Teruggi, who was clearly the brightest among his friends.

I had first met Charlie Horman only recently. One afternoon he showed up unannounced at my apartment door and introduced himself as a friend of some of my friends. That was sufficient basis for us, fueled by a couple of liters of rich Chilean red wine, to talk of politics and life deep into the night. We had a few other sporadic lunches and chats.

Now I can only regret that I did not spend more time with Charlie and Frank. I would next see them a decade later and then only as celluloid ghosts conjured up in the Costa-Gavras film *Missing.*

One young American professor rallied us in Allred's living room and we went as a delegation next door to speak to the US Consul. Enough was enough, we shouted. We wanted the US Embassy to do everything it could to find those who had been arrested. And we wanted protection for ourselves. We wanted the Americans to do what every other diplomatic delegation was doing in Chile – protecting its own citizens from a rampaging, barbarous military. The Consul, Frank Purdy, stood in the hall, blocking access to his office. He spouted the party line: he would look into these matters but there was nothing else to be done that day. The State Department had still issued no specific instructions for Americans in Chile. No special protection was to be extended.

"I recommend you be careful," Consul Purdy said. And then he looked us in the eye and came up with a straight-out lie. "The armed forces are restoring order but there's still a danger of scattered left-wing snipers. Be careful." With that he shooed us out of the Consulate. In retrospect we made mistakes. Our disgust with our government kept us from making what should have been the next logical move. We should have sat down and occupied the Consulate.

That afternoon, shortly after we slumped back from the meeting with the Consul, the whole apartment shook with a thud. Then another bone-chilling thud. Walking out onto Allred's second-floor balcony we saw the two tanks that were doing the shelling. Comfortably squatting in the park, they lobbed artillery rounds into the Fine Arts Campus of the University of Chile across the river. That's how the armed forces of Chile were restoring order.

8pm, Tuesday September 18

One week since the coup, and the call came through from the Mexicans. Thanks to the Mexican government I was to be on a flight organized by the United Nations High Commissioner on Refugees for the next morning. Apart from a special military aircraft that carried Allende's widow to Mexico, this would be the first flight allowed out of Chile. There was a catch, of course. I had to be at the distant Sheraton Hotel the next morning at 7.30 sharp. But curfew didn't lift till 7. It was going to be tight. Nor could I get word to Patricia to meet me to say goodbye. She used a neighbor's phone and if I called her now, at night, it would be too dangerous to defy the curfew. I'd have to wait till morning to call. This was another low point. The mix of emotion I felt was paralyzing. I was ecstatic at the thought I might get out the next day, but terrified that something might go wrong. I was also deeply depressed, laden with survivor's guilt: my only prospect for joy was to flee the slaughterhouse of my friends.

7am, Wednesday September 19

The moment the curfew lifted, I called Patricia and asked her to do what she could to meet me at the Sheraton. I hugged Allred goodbye. With only my passport, $200 in cash, and the borrowed clothes on my back, I walked past the encampment of soldiers outside Allred's door. On the corner, a daring taxi driver was ready for the post-curfew fares. When we got to the Sheraton, I began to reach into my pocket to pay him. The cabbie turned around and commenced one of those skilfully coded dialogues.

"Are you a foreigner?" he asked.

"Yes, an American."

"Have you been living in Chile?" he asked, noting my local accent.

'Yes, for nearly three years."

"Are you leaving today?"

"Yes. I am leaving."

"Then," the cabbie said, "there will be no charge. I want your thoughts about your last moments in Chile to be positive ones."

Operating on a emotional hair-trigger, I couldn't answer through my tears. I only nodded.

Inside the Sheraton lobby I was met by UN and Mexican officials. There was to be a motley mix of about fifty of us on this flight. Few of us knew each other. There were some Spanish clergy. Some Mexican teachers. An American researcher black and blue from a beating. A Texas high-school swim team that had had the bad luck to be passing through Santiago on the wrong day. Because Americans were on the flight manifest, American consular officials were there with clipboards in hand. We refused to talk to them.

Just before I boarded the bus to the airport Patricia arrived for a short goodbye – she would arrange to meet me later in the US. Under heavily armed military escort we were taken to the Cerrillos military airport. After bureaucratic stalling by the junta's new immigration officers, who challenged the validity of our UN-secured safe-conduct pass, we were herded onto a corporate 737 owned by LADECO, one of the copper companies nationalized by Allende.

There was an eerie silence as we took off. No one was sure of anyone else on the flight. As we gained altitude, the plane banked around and began to cross the majestic, snow-sparkled Andes en route to Buenos Aires. Twenty minutes into the flight a crackling voice came over the intercom. "Ladies and gentlemen," the captain announced crisply, "we have just entered Argentine air space."

The entire plane exploded into yelps of joy and applause. Soon we were all on our feet embracing each other, even the Texas swim team. The Kool-Aid and baloney sandwiches that were served remain to this day the best airplane meal I've ever had.

We were greeted in Buenos Aires as heroes even by the immigration police. And that night we marched with 100,000 Argentines to protest the Chilean military dictatorship.

The following week Patricia called me to tell me that on September 22 she went by my apartment and found the front door blown off its hinges, the entire residence sacked by soldiers.

Two months afterwards she came to the US and we have been married ever since. Dennis Allred resigned from the US Foreign Service. Ten years later when I passed through Sweden I found my old guerrilla room-mate Carlos Luna running an import–export business with Cuba.

In his final speech on Magallanes Radio, Salvador Allende promised us that one day there would be a "moral punishment" for the crime and treason that killed him and his Chile. We are still waiting.

Of Salvador Allende, his sacrifice and legacy, Gabriel García Márquez lamented: "His greatest virtue was following through, but fate could only grant him that rare and tragic greatness of dying in armed defense of the whole moth-eaten paraphernalia of an execrable system which he proposed abolishing without a shot."

AFTERMATH: PERPETUAL NIGHT

DECEMBER 1975

As I board the crowded narrow-gauge train that runs from Mendoza, Argentina, to Santiago I must act like I am already in Chile. That country is still 300 miles, nine hours, and an entire mountain range away. But it becomes a reality as soon as I sit down and look at the other travelers cramped in the poorly kept rail car. How many of them might work for General Augusto Pinochet's personal secret police, the DINA?

I escaped Chile two years previously, in part because I was a foreigner, an American who could make some diplomatic connections. But those left behind are writhing in the agony of what has become one of the most vicious of South American political dictatorships. Pinochet's junta has not just moved to dismantle Allende's peaceful revolution. The military regime is also embarked on a full-scale rollback of fifty years of social progress and the re-forging of a "Liberated Chile" in fire and steel.

No one knows the exact death toll. But it is chilling. And with a night-time curfew still in effect twenty-six months after the coup, the feared DINA rule the night – and the day. Their reach extends not only the length of Chile, but beyond its borders where its agents, spies and infiltrators and hired killers collaborate with the intelligence and security services of friendly neighboring regimes.

So as I make this crossing by train over the Andes a few days before Christmas 1975, there is no trace of the usual camaraderie and easy-going sharing of experience found on most South American train journeys. The fact that most on board are going to Chile to visit their families for the holidays, that some of these people undoubtedly fled Chile as I did after the coup, does nothing to lighten the atmosphere.

Six hours into the near silent and nerve-racking ride, we clank and grind to a halt at the sky-high Chilean border. Nobody is to get out, we are told. Instead, the Chilean Immigration Police will be coming on board and will check our papers as the train continues on toward Santiago. And in Chile, the immigration matters are handled not by a special agency but by the plain-clothes Investigative Police, the equivalent of the FBI and CIA.

A foursome of stone-faced, close-cropped cops in tight-fitting suits with penetrating stares methodically take on the task. Chileans are asked to identify themselves by raising their hands and their papers are checked first. A few are being sternly questioned, one twenty-year-old boy in particular: "What's your name? Where do you live? Why are you coming back? What's your name? Where did you work? What's your name? We'll see about you later . . ."

Next are the handful of Argentine, American and European

passports. Just a few, as Pinochet's Chile has hardly become a tourist magnet. The same detective who had been questioning the young man takes my US passport in his hand. My heart sinks and my throat goes dry. Having left Chile in September 1973 as a UN exile, I have been living mostly in Argentina. The word in the Buenos Aires Chilean exile community is that the Chilean state has computerized its watch list at all border entry points. And so to make this trip I have, through my contacts with the Argentine ERP guerrilla group, secured an American passport under a different name. The document I'm traveling with is a real American passport. At least it was when it was manufactured. But now it has been altered to give me a new identity – Michael Errol.

The agent in front of me glances absently at a few pages of the passport, and then without ceremony stamps an entry visa into it, hands it back smiling, and says in passable English, "Welcome, Sir, to Chile."

To the odd tourist who arrives nowadays in Santiago and stays close to the Sheraton, and follows around the English-speaking "guides," and doesn't get caught in the overnight curfew, Chile doesn't look too bad at all. The streets are cleaner than before; the walls of the city, once covered with political slogans, are now whitewashed; and even La Moneda Palace, strafed and rocketed during the coup, has a new and repainted face. Under the facade, the shell marks and bullet pocks can still be discerned, but only if you strain.

After arriving in the capital, I make the decision to visit some former Socialist friends in the workers' shanty-town of Los Pajaritos, not far from the international airport. Along the fifteen-minute bus ride from downtown Santiago to Los Pajaritos I see the first signs of Pinochet's economic program. A dozen unfinished and now abandoned public housing projects.

Los Pajaritos is, in a way, one of those former projects writ large. It's a neighborhood that was born in the fall of 1970, prior to the election of Salvador Allende, when the incumbent President, Eduardo Frei, was doing everything possible to give his centre-right Christian Democratic party a more liberal image. Taking advantage of this temporary waning of authority, more than 200 homeless families, led by grassroots Communist and Socialist Party organizers, seized a large chunk of abandoned fields ten miles to the south of Santiago's civic centre and, throwing up makeshift tents, founded the town. Throughout the following weeks and months, well into the first year of Allende's own Popular Unity government, at least a hundred similar seizures took place.

Two weeks after Allende was inaugurated, his new Ministry of Housing, run by a veteran Communist labor organizer, officially expropriated Los Pajaritos, turned it over to the homeless families, and began to coordinate plans with them for the construction of permanent housing. The settlement, now swollen to 1,500 families, was given government-made wooden shacks to replace the tents until the new homes could be built. In 1973 nearly a million people in Santiago lived in these one- or two-roomed *media aguas*, devoid of either floors or glass windows. Within a year of the initial land seizure, the families of Los Pajaritos, now 2,000 of them, were comfortably installed, at practically no cost to themselves beyond their labor on the project, in their own small brick homes. To these people, the

Allende government was the means of transforming them, almost overnight, from homeless into homeowners.

At the time of Allende's downfall, similar transformations were in progress throughout Santiago, and it was impossible to travel more than a mile or two in any direction without seeing a construction site where new block-type apartments or small homes were being built by and for the 25 per cent of the population that was effectively "houseless" – if not homeless.

Such abandoned worksites stand as decomposing monuments to the junta's economic failures, reminders to Santiago's slum dwellers that, for now, there is no hope of bettering their situation.

Los Pajaritos itself hasn't changed much in these first two years of military rule. The small gardens in front of most of the houses look more neglected than before, but the neat rows of cracker-box houses lining the unpaved streets seem unchanged from September 1973. But while in 1973 the 2,000 families were on their way up – they had new homes, a community clinic, a cooperative dining room, vast popular organizations took care of food distribution, child care, and education – their lives today have been reduced to a struggle for day-to-day survival. The popular organizations are outlawed, their leaders in jail, the clinic has been closed down, 65 per cent of the heads of families are out of work, and the cooperative dining room, long gone, has been replaced by a church-sponsored emergency soup kitchen that is fighting to provide the neighborhood children with at least one spartan dish of food each day.

"The starving out of these people doesn't seem to be enough for the junta," complains a European priest working in the neighborhood. "Now they are being forced out of these homes that cost them so much to attain." The military government's housing department notified the dwellers of all such Allende-built homes that the almost insignificant weekly payment, a type of government mortgage, was now being raised 500 per cent and that the number of payments registered had to total 485 by December 31, or they would be turned out into the streets. Most households have no more than 175 or 200 payments in and have already been evicted. A few days later the vacated homes are already occupied by new families, and in every case they are families of officers of the Federal Police. One woman lamented, "By February we will owe more than 350 payments: we can't pay it; nobody can. We are trying to organize to stop the evictions, but now it is harder than ever because we have these cops, these vultures, living right among us." *El Mercurio*, the Chilean daily that most ardently supports the junta and, as we know from the lips of Richard Helms, received copious amounts of those CIA destabilizing dollars, was forced to write in a recent edition: "Street begging, especially in downtown Santiago, has risen sharply. Young mothers, often with two or three children at their sides, can be found begging in front of every major building or office. The children begin to play by asking for coins."

And it isn't just little children who are out roaming the streets trying to survive. Church sources estimate that, in spite of the 1am curfew, there are now more prostitutes working in Santiago than ever before: somewhere between 15,000 and 20,000.

The entertainment and sports industry of the country has been wiped out. This is a product of the disastrous economic situation and the nightly curfew. The Chilean Actors' and Musicians' Union reports that, as of October 1975, 96 per cent of their membership was out of work. Most of the city's night-clubs have been closed down. A few, notably in the two IT&T-owned Sheraton Hotels, seem to be staying above water, thanks to the straggle of tourists who still drift through town. An evening in one of these *boîtes* costs more than the monthly salary of a worker.

More than 100 cinemas throughout the country have had to close their doors. Rigorous government censorship has kept films of any social significance from entering the country, and the usual fare is limited to Italian Westerns, Spanish musicals, and American disaster films like *Jaws* and *The Towering Inferno*. *Fiddler on the Roof* was banned in 1975 for being "pro-Communist," but this is no surprise from a government that claims the United States Senate is controlled by "Marxist–Leninists."

The infamous National Stadium, known to the world as the junta's first concentration camp, now stands vacant during even the most important soccer matches. It is a rare occasion when more than 3,000 people show up, this in a stadium of 80,000 seats. In a recent B-League match, a world record was no doubt established when only seventeen fans bought tickets to watch twenty-two men on the field contest the game. Nobody has any money to do anything, except maybe feed themselves.

Economically, this year of 1975 has been the junta's worst. And 1976 promises to be even bleaker. The junta has shown no willingness to abandon its "social market economy," that fiscal Frankenstein fathered by Professor Milton Friedman of the

University of Chicago. Friedman, who to date has found no government more willing than Chile's to let him "experiment," has made repeated trips to Santiago to counsel the junta on the finer points of his laissez-faire program. The professor insists that if the government abstains from intervention in the economy, except, of course, for limiting wages, smashing unions, and jailing and killing their leaders, production will rise, inflation will fall, and the economy will be "guided by that invisible hand, the free market place." At the end of 1975, production was down 20 per cent against the previous year, essential imports fell 100 per cent, the buying power of the consumer fell 55 per cent, inflation was still at 375 per cent a year, and as the final result of Friedman's shock treatment, official unemployment stood at more than 17 per cent, though most observers, not least the Church, place the real figure at closer to 25 per cent.

The new economic measures include the now customary increases in the price of consumer items: rice, sugar, flour, meat, cooking oil and transport. In the majority of cases the hikes ran in the area of 70 to 100 per cent over the former prices. Wages were increased by 32 per cent, a figure so inadequate that even the junta-controlled labor organizations rebelled. Though under the leadership of men handpicked by Pinochet, twenty-seven miners' federations rejected the offer and asked instead for a 300 per cent increase.

Carlos Ossa, an exiled Chilean journalist in Buenos Aires, summed up the situation in the Argentine publication *Crisis*: "Never before have so many gotten so poor so fast and arrived all at the same time at the point of collapse."

Fear for one's personal security in Santiago is a daily preoccupation. Though the number of uniformed police and soldiers on the streets is unremarkable, what people fear most are the detectives, the agents of the three branches of military intelligence, and the newly created DINA, an organization responsible to President Pinochet alone which reigns over the population, and the other intelligence services, as a sort of Chilean Gestapo.

A close friend of mine who held a ministerial-level post under Allende was arrested in late 1975. I arrange to meet him under rather cloak-and-dagger conditions. A well-born, fine-featured scion of the Chilean bourgeoisie, he sends me a message to meet him in a dingy working-class café far from the center of town. When I arrive, I hardly recognize him. Gaunt and pale, his eyes are now set in deep, dark sockets. After not seeing him for two years, I have an urge to hug him, but he motions me away. As we sit across a small table, he speaks quietly, hesitantly. He is more humiliated than angry as he recounts his travails: "Six uniformed police broke my door down at seven in the morning . . . Two minutes later I was near unconscious, had a broken rib, was blindfolded, and was riding between two of them in the back seat of a car. Twenty minutes later I was taken out, slugged around some more, and pushed into a cell, blindfolded and bleeding. About five hours passed and then I was dragged to another room, had my blindfold removed and saw that I was in the presence of two plain-clothes men. They told me I was in the Tacna army regiment headquarters, that they were from the DINA, and that I had to tell them immediately who I was in contact with abroad. Five minutes later I was stripped and tied to a metal bedframe, water was poured all over me, and electrodes were connected to my nipples. They alternated questions with threats and escalating amounts of voltage. Later they applied current to my ears and tongue, which hurt the most, and, of course, to my genitals."

At this point, his narrative pauses. He takes a sip of beer. And I sit motionless. I want to cry. But what do I have to cry about? It was he, not I, who was strapped down to "la Parilla" – what the torturers and their prey alike call "the Grill." And after this brief meeting, we both know I will return to the daylight of a more civilized world while my shattered friend will sleep in fear every night.

The Grill, of course, is only one form of torture imported from the earlier dictatorship in Brazil and now being refined and institutionalized in Chile. There's also "the Submarine," systematic near-drowning, and "the Perch," which suspends the victim in a nerve-crushing posture. Electrodes in the nose, the mouth, the vagina. Live rats inserted in the vagina. The rape of children or wives in front of their loved ones. Broken fingers, shattered ribs, smashed legs and elbows. Mock executions and real ones.

My friend continues: "When I passed out they would revive me, have a doctor check me, wait an hour or so, and then start all over again. This went on for a week. I was finally released, thanks to friends who are ambassadors. But how many people can count diplomats among their closest friends?"

There isn't even the pretense of the rule of law in Chile. All civil rights have been lifted. Habeas corpus isn't recognized. Citizens can be and are arrested by uniformed or plain-clothes police, or troops, or security agents, or death squads or what the press politely calls "unknown armed men in civilian clothes." Someone detained can wake up in criminal court or before an all-powerful military tribunal or not at all. A prisoner can be taken to jail or can languish in a "clandestine jail," a DINA torture center. Bodies can be dumped on the doorstep of their families, into the sea, into an unmarked grave, a hastily dug lime pit, an abandoned coal mine, or simply made to disappear.

The press and the TV ask no questions. They only celebrate law and order.

But two years after the coup, there is no order in Chile. Peace and quiet is only found in the cemetery. I find it impossible to reconstruct my old social network. Of my former friends, the fortunate ones have fled to Italy, France, Spain or Scandinavia. Some are still in hiding, others are unaccounted for, probably dead. A couple are detained in military camps, and there are those, incredibly, who are unscathed – just permanently traumatized. Finally, there are those, I am told, whom I should look up only at my own risk. They have undergone a *cambio de chaqueta*, a changing of stripes, a switching of sides.

Neither the factories, farms, schools, nor universities are exempt from the presence of the DINA. In any institution where Chileans congregate either to study or work, a self-imposed and discreet silence is observed. In the university classroom a student must be careful of the statements she makes and the questions she asks, lest she be uncovered as an "extremist." In the high schools once effervescent with political activity, civilian principals have been replaced by active military officers.

In the factories, independent unions are banned, collective bargaining is banned, requests for higher salaries are banned and, as one factory worker told me, "You cannot even open your mouth to complain, to let off steam. If you do and are unlucky, the DINA will hear of it and off you go! If you are lucky, then only some worker who wants to get close to the boss will hear you and you will be out of a job . . . there are five guys waiting in line to replace any of us."

Human rights groups, operating only in the shadows, have struggled to compile lists of those killed or jailed by the junta. So many people have just "disappeared" that no one can make any accurate count. All we know is that the bloody, ferocious repression unleashed by Pinochet in the first hours of his regime has still not peaked. The night of terror grows darker in Chile and there is still no sight of dawn.

As many as 400,000 people, from a population of 10 million, have already left the country since September 1973, and long lines continue to form in front of the passport office, where the simplest task can drag on for months.

The deteriorated economic situation, and the government's hard-headed refusal to rectify it, has eroded the junta's support among the small merchants, the professional classes and even the small- and medium-sized industrialists. The continuing and flagrant violation of human rights has brought the government to a showdown with the powerful Catholic Church, not to mention ninety-six countries within the United Nations. Normally tame sectors of the Christian Democratic party, "in recess,' have also begun to rebel and there has been of late a resurfacing of activity by the left-wing parties and underground organizations.

The junta's longtime tacit supporter, ex-President Frei, another recipient of those CIA funds, recently turned his back on the regime, and went so far as to accuse the generals of being "Fascists." Patricio Aylwin, who, along with Frei, controls the right-wing sector of the Christian Democrats, also leveled some strong Christmas-time attacks against the junta. This might be seen as rats abandoning a sinking ship, but these are some very important rats. In most Latin American capitals, it is understood that Frei and Aylwin are now the key men in the State Department's plans for Chile. Tired of being embarrassed by the barely literate crew today in charge of Santiago, the US is opting for a pact between more "moderate" military men and "responsible civilian elements," i.e., the right-wing Christian Democrats. This, as Kissinger no doubt dreams, would give birth to a new military government with a human face, one that would then call limited elections (the Left remaining outlawed) so that Mr. Frei could once again lead a "democratic Chile" back into the good graces of the West.

But General Pinochet continues to consolidate his power. There was originally some notion that he might be merely a sort of administrative chairman of the four-man junta. But by now he has concentrated power in his hands and he is very much the traditional *caudillo*. Just recently, Admiral José Merino, one of the original members of the four-man junta, was suddenly replaced by another representative of the Navy. Merino's political demise came, according the junta, as a result of a "lingering heart disease." But most of Chile observers discount this explanation and see the Admiral's fall as a simple result of a political purge. This reporter agrees, having seen the Admiral play a brisk game of golf at the Viña del Mar Country Club just a few days before his removal.

A further demonstration of Pinochet's accelerated consolidation of power was the reshuffling of the presidential cabinet in the first week of March. Pinochet sacked a number of his ministers and replaced them with new military men.

But mostly, Pinochet's rule is about extending the terror. Back in the first days of the coup when I was holed up in Dennis Allred's apartment, I remember him getting a visit from one of the fair-haired children of the Right, someone I will call Enrique. A member of the far-right Nationalist Youth, he had just come from watching his friends sack the Communist Party Central Committee Headquarters. Enrique was lugging around a trophy – a paperweight looted from the desk of hunted CP General Secretary Luis Corvalán. As we sat and sipped coffee, Enrique fondled the brass object and mused out loud: "All Chileans are deluded. Allende thought there was something you could call Chilean-style military government – one that will be short-lived, moderate, not very bloody and one that will in six months turn power back over to us civilians. But they are just as wrong as Allende was. Pinochet will wind up being like every other South American dictator, maybe worse."

Enrique's words have been prophetic. Today, the most important political force in Chile is not the right-wing parties that opposed Allende. It is Pinochet's DINA. Last year they successfully hunted down and annihilated the leadership of the extreme left MIR, the Movement of the Revolutionary Left that had been mounting a feeble armed resistance. Its leader, Miguel Enriquez, the dashing son of Allende's former education minister, was cornered in a suburban safe house and riddled with bullets. The Socialist Youth leadership was also targeted and destroyed. So were the Young Communists, the Central Workers' Federation, the Chilean student federations, the farm workers' leagues, the neighborhood associations, the journalists' guild, university professors' association and many others.

As I board the train to return to Argentina, I leave behind me a Chile still in the grip of a homicidal spasm. Pinochet and the military, to the applause of the Chilean Right, and with the nodding approval of the Nixon administration, staged their 1973 coup in the name of liberating Chile from Marxian socialism. But under the overthrown Socialist government of Salvador Allende, a liberal constitution was fully in force. A vibrant private sector dominated the economy. A fully functional Congress was controlled by the conservative opposition. A dozen daily newspapers, from far right to extreme left flourished free of all censorship. Not one Chilean was in jail for political crimes. Freedom of speech and assembly was fully respected. Allende's election had enriched, not atrophied democracy.

And now the junta that has overthrown him in the name of freedom is constructing a regime every bit as noxious – and in many ways worse – than the Stalinist governments of which it claims to be the antithesis. The Congress has been padlocked, the free press trashed and burned along with the courts and the political system itself, all opposition is banned, and those suspected of resistance are hunted down, tortured, beaten, dismembered, assassinated, and "disappeared." Pinochet's patrons in the White House and State Department, and those in the ideologically blinkered media establishment who were so horrified by Allende's nationalization of the US-owned copper mines, can barely bring themselves to hiccup a protest over what they call the "excesses" of the Pinochet dictatorship. He's a sonofabitch for sure. But he's "our" sonofabitch. His defenders and apologists in Washington point to his free-market policies as proof positive they have backed the right horse. But it's really the mounting body count that stands as the most fitting monument to the first two years of achievement of the military regime. And sitting atop it all, his arms crossed over his chest, his lips clamped together, his eyes hidden behind pitch-black lenses, is, indeed, the Liberator of Chile, General Augusto Pinochet Ugarte.

RESISTANCE: STREETS OF FIRE

SEPTEMBER 1983

On the afternoon of September 11 1983, the tenth anniversary of General Pinochet's coup, the Chilean national soccer team was squaring off against that of another dictatorship – Uruguay. For a few hours, politics would be put aside as 60,000 fans followed the match inside Santiago's National Stadium and hundreds of thousands more tuned in via the military government's Chilean National Television.

But with barely twenty minutes left in the game, and with the Chilean team leading 2–0, more than half the fans in the stadium suddenly stood up and, stealing the tune of a popular sports jingle, began to sing in unison: "It's going to fall! It's going to fall! The military dictatorship is going to fall!"

The sound of the protest song reverberating around the soccer field was a far cry from the rat-tat-tat of the executioners' machine guns and the screams of the tortured that ten years ago had made this same stadium an international symbol of terror and human degradation.

It was a sign that something very important was happening in Chile.

Most Chileans will tell you that *el gran cambio*, the big change, can be dated to three months ago – to May 11 1983. It was then that huge numbers of people, the poor and the middle class as well, joined in the first Day of National Protest against the Pinochet regime. Since then, the monthly protests have mushroomed in scope and tone. A new political opposition has been fashioned. Critical magazines and radio stations have begun to blossom. And the slums and shanty-towns, the *poblaciones* and *campamentos* that ring Santiago and house one-third of its population, now seethe with resistance and rebellion.

The names of the most insurgent zones – La Victoria, La Legua, Lo Hermida – have acquired an almost legendary aura among opposition and government forces alike. During the days of protest, reporters, activists, police agents, and the population in general awaited "combat" reports from these "conflictive areas" which in more ordinary times elicit no more attention than any other urban slum.

No wonder that these, the most marginal of neighborhoods, have become the incubators of the first acts of mass resistance to the Pinochet dictatorship. While a workers' average buying power has fallen steadily since the 1973 coup, the decline has been steepest among the poorest sectors of the population. A Chilean subsisting on the government's Minimum Employments Program – and some 600,000 families do – has to spend an entire day's salary to buy just over a kilo of bread.

"Sometimes I go to the bakery and see a father of five ask to buy only three rolls," says Father David Murphy, a British priest working in the slums of Maipu. "There is real hunger here and now it has become explosive."

Entering La Legua from Santa Rosa Avenue I find it hard to believe that Pinochet's Moneda Palace is only a ten-minute drive away. The walls of this most notorious of Chilean shanty-towns bleed with bold graffiti: "Long Live the Popular Rebellion! Pinochet: Your Days Are Numbered!"

The street signs and traffic signals have all been uprooted and were consumed in last month's impromptu barricades. The intersections are filled with the dark rings burned into the asphalt by blazing tires. When a group of idle youth spot my car, made conspicuous by foreign press markings, they surround it. And when I roll down the window, they grab for my microphone and shout: "Tell the truth! We are hungry and want jobs. Let them kill us. It makes no difference."

"Give us some fucking guns," says another youth. "We can't fight these assholes with our bare hands. We need guns!"

Father Guido Peteers, a Belgian priest working here since 1972, says the kids of La Legua "may in fact already be arming themselves." Pamphlets on how to make Molotov cocktails and pipe bombs have circulated for months in the area, he says. "The process here is over-riding all of the political parties. It's becoming uncontrollable. These people want the dictatorship out now."

Later that night, as this month's Day of National Protest was concluding, the pungent odor from barricades of burning tires chokes the air of La Legua. Every intersection has been blocked since early afternoon. Large groups are marching up and down the streets calling for the overthrow of Pinochet. The crowds swell toward 8pm and the bonfires blaze bright. And then, exactly on the hour, Chileans here in La Legua and throughout the country start banging on pots and pans.

The sound is deafening and the images before my eyes evoke some magic realist scene from the mind of García Márquez. The dirt streets teem with thousands frenetically beating not only on pots and pans but also on lead pipes, wash tubs, stop signs, bus stops, coffee pots, any two pieces of metal available. In the surreal orange glow of the bonfires and the few remaining mercury-vapor street lamps, here are young and old, most of them poorly clad, some barefoot, some standing, others kneeling, all intently pounding metal against metal, all engaged in a feverish quasi-ritual exorcism of the military. The pounding is accompanied by the rhythmic, almost primal chant of "Bread! Work! Justice! Freedom!"

Around the bonfires and under banners hand-painted with the portrait of Salvador Allende, teenage boys and girls, their faces covered with bandanas, stand guard with slingshots and sharpened wooden poles and speak of becoming Chilean "sandinistas." Many around the fires are barely adolescent, probably infants or toddlers at the time of the 1973 coup and Allende's death.

"Who was Salvador Allende?" I ask a boy no older than twelve.

"He was *ours*! The President of the poor – that's why they killed him."

"They don't teach you that in school."

"I don't go to school," the boy says. "But I know all about Allende. Our parents tell us. He died for us. And now we are ready to die too if we have to."

A handful of the boy's *compadres* listening in to our dialogue pick up on the cue and begin chanting in unison: "We will die fighting, but never of hunger!"

It's not just the poor who swell with anger and rebellion. Many of the lighter-skinned Chilean middle class – ten years ago fervent supporters of Pinochet's dictatorship – now feel betrayed by the General's regime. Economically ruined, their businesses and professions shut down, their children unable to find jobs or afford university tuition, they have seen their dreams of prospering under military tutelage turn into a nightmare.

A popular joke makes the rounds in the creamy middle-class suburb of Providencia: At the height of border tensions with Argentina a few years back, General Pinochet tells his top army commander to assemble "an elite destruction force." A week later the commander takes Pinochet to a swank hotel suite, and shows him two dozen clean-cut young men, blue-eyed, dressed in Brooks Brothers suits, all with matching attaché cases. They are all reading the *Wall Street Journal* or punching away at their hand-held calculators.

"What the hell is this?" Pinochet barks. "I wanted a force of destroyers!"

"Why, yes, sir," his commander snaps back. "Here they are, sir. Everyone knows twenty Chicago Boys can destroy any country overnight."

Indeed, the decade of University of Chicago-inspired monetarism that shaped Pinochet's economic policies has turned Chile into an unmitigated failure. The economic collapse has greatly increased in the last two years and is certainly the catalyst behind the recent wave of rebellion. As one middle-class accountant tells me: "Augusto Pinochet has accomplished two things that Salvador Allende never could. First, he has united the entire country – against him, of course. And second, General Pinochet has single-handedly managed to wipe out Chilean private enterprise."

The Pinochet liberal-import policy has, in fact, forced the closure of thousands of Chilean firms, cutting domestic production capacity in half over the past decade. A Central Bank report lists 431 major industrial bankruptcies in 1981, 810 in 1982 and more than 400 in the first half of this year. Over the past decade, unemployment has risen to a numbing 30 per cent. And the average jobless rate since 1973 has floated at around 18 per cent – three times higher than the average during the previous twenty years. In a recent poll by the University of Chile conducted among the unemployed living in central Santiago, 2,500 respondents listed their last job as "executive." Nineteen thousand others as "professional."

My Chilean cousin Pepe, who lives in the privileged enclave of Las Condes with his wife and twenty-three-year-old son, counts himself lucky. He has held on to his job as a personnel officer for a foreign-owned mining company. But his wife, Silvia, has had for the first time to take a job as a door-to-door collection agent for one of the brokerages which now run Chile's privatized social security system.

Dinner at Pepe's is certainly superior to the fare in the impoverished *poblaciones*. But even here, in the confines of the solidly middle class, the crunch is being felt. As the guest at the dinner table, I am offered the one pork chop; the rest of the family eats a more proletarian serving of spaghetti. Soon an argument breaks out between Pepe and his son, Miguel, the father arguing that it is time for the boy to go out and find a part-time job. Miguel responds that he cannot because he must study, because there are few such part-time jobs, and because even if he did find one his fellow middle-class friends would ridicule him.

The family dispute is mercifully interrupted by the doorbell. A young man wearing a Lacoste sweater and carrying a small metal basket conducts a swift negotiation with Silvia, who returns with a few eggs and a hunk of cheese. She explains the boy is from a well-to-do family down the street who is picking up extra money peddling dairy products. When I ask why that isn't frowned upon by the neighbors while Miguel taking a part-time job in, say, a restaurant would be, Silvia strains to convince me that the boy wasn't really selling the eggs out of need. "His uncle is a big landowner," she says. "He was just offering the eggs as a convenience to the neighbors."

Pepe loudly snorts out his incredulity. "Please," he says. The kid's just one more "disguised jobless." The dinner conversation turns to what kind of job opportunities there might be for Miguel in the United States.

Just what course the protests of the last few months may take remains unclear. Those opposed to the dictatorship are finding their first public voice after a solid decade of unrelenting terror. Banging on pots and pans and milling around burning tires with wooden spears does not challenge the structure of the dictatorship. The bubbling discontent has translated itself into two new fledgling opposition political fronts: one of the center, the other more leftist. Both fronts are trying to channel the popular outrage into organized campaigns of massive civil disobedience. And the debate between the two fronts is now open and raging: negotiate with Pinochet for more political freedom or, as some sectors of the Left argue, make this country ungovernable as long as the military remains in power?

While the opposition remains divided and uncertain, Pinochet has not flinched in responding to the upsurge of resistance with steely repression. During the organized protests of these last few months, heavily armed contingents of several hundred *carabineros* have rampaged through the shanty-towns, smashing windows and furniture, dumping tear gas into homes, shooting at unarmed civilians, and rounding up hundreds in mass arrests. To face last month's National Day of Protest, Pinochet threw a staggering 18,000 army troop reinforcement into the streets of the capital.

In one high-profile incident this month, a squad of uniformed riot police, riding in a civilian bus without license plates, pulled to a stop on the main avenue bordering La Victoria slum. Residents of the area saw at least two cops get out of the vehicle, stand behind a street sign, and begin to fire indiscriminately at those who passed within range. Twenty-one-year-old Miguel Angel Zavala caught one of those bullets in his neck and bled to death on the ground as the police drove off in the unmarked bus.

When, an hour after the killing, I go with a group of six other reporters to look into what happened, we immediately find the bus described by the locals: it is filled with police riot shields and parked in front of a police command post. We start to take pictures of the vehicle when a group of police come pouring out of the post and arrest us.

"You are in preventive detention until we determine just what you are doing," says the desk sergeant. "You are not allowed to attack military or police installations with your cameras."

"That bus we were looking at had no military markings on it," I counter. "It is a civilian bus without license plates."

"That's *not* a civilian bus," the sergeant snaps back. "It's not a military vehicle either. It's not military or civilian. That bus is of no interest to anyone."

Two hours of tense negotiations conducted by the auxiliary archbishop of Santiago – alerted by a priest who saw us arrested – secure our release after we are warned never again to take any pictures around police stations.

The next afternoon, 10,000 protesters and mourners accompany young Zavala's body to the Metropolitan Cemetery.

As we march along the Pan-American highway in Santiago's gritty southern quarter, thousands more spontaneously swell our ranks. Outside the cemetery gates a ring of heavily armed *carabineros* stand ready. Two small police tanks squat in front of us. The crowd marches peacefully and quietly into the burial grounds.

I stand with a friend at the edge of the open grave where Zavala is to be buried. But as his simple wooden coffin is lowered into the ground, the police begin firing barrage after barrage of tear gas into our ranks. One canister lands obscenely on top of Zavala's still uncovered coffin. We disperse, wildly gasping for breath. The police surround the cemetery and then unleash several volleys of rubber bullets that ricochet off the forest of headstones in a macabre fashion. A reporter from the French daily *Libération* is beaten unconscious by the cops. A CNN cameraman takes a rubber bullet in the chest and goes sprawling.

But this is now routine in Pinochet's Chile. The Chilean Human Rights Commission has held a number of press conferences at which dozens of the poor have testified to the regular doses of violence applied in the *poblaciones*, the systematic torture in police command posts and still continuing arrests and disappearances. One human rights worker describes the pattern of repression as "a series of *Kristallnachts*. Here in Chile, the ghettos are the *poblaciones*, the shanty-towns. Being Jewish isn't the crime, being poor is."

On the morning following the attack at the cemetery, the director of Santiago's emergency health service admits that his facilities have been "exhausted" by the number of injured and wounded. At the Church-sponsored Vicarate of Solidarity I literally have to step over the wounded to gain access to meet with Dr. Mario Insunza. He says he has registered more than 225 people coming into the office that morning seeking medical help. "Many won't go to the public hospitals," he says. "They're afraid they would face even more reprisals."

As violent as the political conflict has become in Chile, there are few in the opposition – whether centrists or leftists – who believe that any definitive showdown is looming on the immediate horizon. They speak of Chilean "exceptionalism," the "professional nature" of the armed forces, the "passive" temper of the Chilean people, the "capacity" of the Chilean political class to negotiate. For weeks this Chilean winter I listened to argument after argument as to why a full-blown rebellion or insurgency could not materialize in Chile.

I had heard these same sorts of arguments passionately spelled out a decade before – in a different context – during Allende's last days. I had heard all of the reasons why a violent coup could never take place in Chile, I heard them right up to the morning of September 11 1973 when the doors were kicked in, the "subversives" dragged away, the radio stations dynamited, the factories overrun and occupied by Chilean marines, the *poblaciones* strafed with machine guns and ringed with tanks, and the national traditions of 150 years of democracy consumed by the walls of flame and billowing columns of smoke belched forth from the bombed-out Moneda Palace.

ILLUSION: A TRANSVESTITE DEMOCRACY

JANUARY–MARCH 1998

Memory, in a country like Chile, in a country which has survived its own massacre, is always unpleasant, and certainly, nowadays, unpopular. And yet the raucous demonstrations I witness unfolding in front of the now-reconstructed La Moneda Presidential Palace this winter can't help but remind me of some of the more glorious moments I witnessed here twenty-five years ago when I worked inside the palace as a young translator to President Allende.

The immense Constitution Plaza that yawns in front of the Moneda was back then so often the stage upon which tens and sometimes hundreds of thousands of ordinary Chileans would march and rally around the ideas and programs that then seemed the touchstone of a new and still unfolding era: a nation taking control of its destiny, breaking free from dependence, reclaiming its natural resources, empowering and transferring wealth to the poor, daring to construct a democratic socialism. For me and many others of my generation, what we saw in the plazas and streets of Allende's Chile, coming in the wake of the French '68, the hot Italian autumn of '69, the American student strike of '70, promised to ignite a new time of optimism and radical renewal.

We were, of course, wrong. The last massive demonstration I attended in this Plaza was on September 4 1973, the third anniversary of Allende's election, when a half-million Chilean workers, knowing the end was near, marched in front of a sombre-looking President and vociferously pleaded for weapons. But it was far too late.

Chile was not the prelude to my generation's accomplishments. Rather, it was our political high water mark. The Chilean military coup of 1973 was merely the overture to the devil's symphony that marked the massacres in Cambodia and East Timor, the Argentine dirty war, the scorched earth campaigns in Guatemala and El Salvador, the CIA assassination manuals in Nicaragua, the rise of Thatcherism in Europe, the Reagan–Bush counter-revolution here at home.

That is why I am so intrigued by the three, four, sometimes five thousand social security workers who have been regularly flooding into downtown Santiago this winter, throwing leaflets into the air, chanting and stomping and whistling, chaining themselves to lightposts and church pews, blocking traffic and standing up to riot-police water cannons and tear-gas barrages. It certainly looks like the same gumption that drove Chilean workers to demand guns from Allende to face down the military.

But there's an ugly glitch in this scenario. This is the Chile of 1998. And like so much in modern Chile, this demonstration is an illusion. These workers aren't fighting for a free pint of milk for every Chilean infant, or for nationalization of the copper mines, for a higher minimum wage or for union control of the workplace. No, these workers – men and women alike – are the salaried and commissioned sales force of Chile's privatized social security pension system. And they are infuriated by a very mild proposed government rule change that is aimed at curbing the rampant fraud which riddles the system. If approved, the new rule would add a thin layer of protection to all Chilean workers. But it would also directly bite into the monthly commissions the protesting workers have been earning by juggling others' pension funds. Indeed, these workers in the streets today are battling for the right to keep ripping off their fellow workers. It's a long road to have come in twenty-five years. The more I become entwined with Chile, the less I recognize it.

Allende triumphed in Chile precisely because, long before his election, a century-old tradition of parliamentary democracy and advanced social legislation had forged a society that prided itself on advanced public discourse, a national commitment to mutual aid and solidarity, and what seemed – even under conservative administration – a permanent sense of social justice. But that Chile has vanished into collective amnesia. Today, after seventeen years of military dictatorship and eight years of "democracy," what passes for the Left is complicit in managing a grotesque system that allows murderers to walk free and torturers to be elected to national office, that boasts one of the most unequal economic systems in the world, where even public schools are privatized. Chile, perhaps more than anywhere else on earth, is a place where idolatry of the market has most deeply penetrated.

Chile hardly holds a patent on a pullback from politics – a

reflex now rampant from Peoria to Poland. But few, if any, countries in recent decades have regressed quite as far as Chile. In Eastern Europe the economic systems were stood on their heads, but decades of Stalinist cynicism and duplicity served to grease the way for the savageries of frontier capitalism.

Chile was different. In 1970, on the eve of Allende's election, one American researcher found Chilean teenagers – along with their Israeli and Cuban counterparts – to be among the least alienated, most optimistic youth in the world. But seventeen years of military dictatorship and a quarter of a century of the most orthodox application of sink-or-swim social policy have imposed a collective neurosis on Chile – it has driven its people crazy, driven them to market.

Chilean mill workers now assiduously follow daily stock quotes to make sure their private pensions will be there when they retire. When their children leave the school gates, they stick velcro-backed insignias from elite academies onto their uniforms, lest the other subway rider think they go to more downscale institutions. Bookstores that once brimmed with political classics now stock huge piles of translations of Anthony Robbins and other quick-road-to-success gurus. National "educational" TV features training films in entrepreneurship and good customer relations. Prime-time infomercials beam dubbed-over blue-eyed gringos blissfully hawking Smart Choppers and Sure Fire Bass Lures into the rural and fishing villages of the Chilean south, where horses are still sometimes a preferred means of transportation.

A recent police checkpoint in the posh Vitacura neighborhood found that a high percentage of drivers ticketed for using their cell phones while in motion were using toy – even wooden – replicas. Other middle-class motorists bake with their windows closed pretending they have air conditioning. Workers at the ritzy Jumbo supermarket complain that, on Saturday mornings, the dressed-to-kill clientele fill their carts high with delicacies, parade them in front of the Joneses, and then discretely abandon them before having to pay. In the upmarket La Dehesa neighborhood, Florida palm trees are pouring in and black butlers are all the rage. Stocky six-foot Dominicans are the preferred choice: the first wave of imported help, from Peru, turned out to be unfashionably short-statured. In the rickety shanty-towns around Santiago, Diners Club cards are used to charge potatoes and cabbage, while Air Jordans and Wonder-Bras are bought on twelve-month installment plans.

Yes, a few lonely souls still protest the disappearances, murders, and thousands of unprosecuted barbarities of the past two-and-a-half decades. But they are denounced as threats to stability, provocateurs, losers, dinosaurs of the past, as are nearly all reminders of the way Chile's new commercial culture has been grafted onto a body politic charred to the bone.

And yet, for all the striving to forget, for all the frenzied talk about being an "economic Jaguar," about modernization and a global future, Chile cannot escape its past. On this coming March 11, the man who embodies Chile's darkest history, the 800-pound Gorilla of Chilean politics, eighty-two-year-old Captain General Augusto Pinochet, gives up his post as Commander of the Army and takes up his new seat as unelected, but fully empowered, Senator for Life. Indeed, under a constitution his regime wrote in 1980 which allows for a certain number of appointed senators, former military commanders will now constitute the single biggest "party" caucus in the Senate. And with a two-thirds majority congressional vote required to enact serious reforms, Senator Pinochet will, until he dies, effectively hold the power of political veto in his hands.

Pinochet's continuing prominence in Chile is more emblem than aberration. His dictatorship may have been voted out of office by the plebiscite of 1988. But it is his economic and political model that has triumphed. For the American media, the Chile story is, as always, a neat and simple tale: bloody dictator forced by history to wipe out Communism gets voted out and a civilian government leads the transition to democracy while retaining a free-market economic system.

But reality is more complicated. In Chile there has been no transition, nor will there be one in the foreseeable future. What we see instead in Chile is the consolidation of a new global model – a model that premièred here twenty-five years ago in an orgy of death and fire and has since been ever refined and better marketed. A model that, in some form of another, is being proposed for all of us. "Chile is what I call a transvestite democracy," says Chilean sociologist Tomás Moulian. "She looks like a nice friendly young lady. But lift up her skirts, and you're in for a big surprise."

The *New York Times* recently celebrated this state of affairs by crediting Pinochet with a "coup that began Chile's transformation from a backwater banana republic to the economic star of Latin America." Leaving aside the fact that the pre-Pinochet "banana republic" produced a bumper crop of world-renowned artists, scientists, and intellectuals, including two Nobel Prizes for Literature, the *Times* has also got it wrong on the economy. The 7 per cent annual growth since 1986 cited by enthusiasts of the Chilean model ignores several other less attractive figures: there was no growth between 1973 and 1986; real salaries have declined 10 per cent since 1986 and are still 18 per cent lower than they were during the Allende period. One quarter of the country lives in absolute poverty and a third of the nation earns less than $30 a week.

A recent study by the World Bank of sixty-five countries ranked Chile as seventh worst in unequal income distribution, side by side with Kenya and Zimbabwe. To get a notion of just how skewed this is, consider that in the US 70 per cent of national income goes to workers and 30 per cent to capital. In Chile, 40 per cent goes to workers and 60 per cent to capital. The top 10 per cent of the population earns almost half the wealth. "The 100 richest people in Chile earn more than the state spends on all social services," says Senator Jorge Lavanderos.

Chile is a classic case for growth without development. But as Canadian economist Phillip Oxhorn has noted, the big difference between the poor of the past and the poor of today is that the latter now have to work. "Therefore economic growth by itself will not solve problems of poverty and inequality," he says. "It will only reproduce them."

Defenders of the Chilean model say these inequalities are a small and acceptable price to pay for a system that rewards individual initiative. "We have extraordinary success because this system was applied without any political opposition," say US-trained economist Jaime Vargas. "People know the rules of the game and have to believe in themselves. People are not into politics and not into any groups of any kind – unions, clubs, whatever. Chile," he says proudly, "is a world of incredible individualism."

Radical economist Orlando Caputo has a more clinical view. "The Chilean system is easy to understand. Over the past twenty years $60 billion dollars has been transferred from salaries to profits."

The belt of tin-roofed shanty-towns that house a quarter of Santiago's four million residents pulsated with Allende supporters during his brief tenure and then became a fiery necklace of resistance to the dictatorship. The military eventually bulldozed the Che Guevara and New Havana settlements. And Pinochet "eradicated" 200,000 shanty-town dwellers and relocated them to new slums in the chilly Andean foothills. But other neighborhoods took up the mantle of intransigent opposition: La Bandera, La Legua, Pudahuel and especially La Victoria.

Since its birth on a land squat in 1957, La Victoria has incubated two generations of radical activists and revolutionaries. During the protests and confrontations of the mid-1980s, La Victoria was on the front line. Armed troops shot dead the community priest, Andrés Jarlan, when they opened fire on a group of reporter friends of mine. His successor, Pierre Dubois, was deported to France. In defiance of military rule, La Victoria's main artery, Avenida 30 de Octubre, would be covered with Siqueiros-like murals denouncing the regime's soldiers as assassins. On the eve of planned protests, the dictatorship would ring La Victoria with literally thousands of troops and, if confidence was high enough, would rip the neighbor-hood apart with house-to-house searches.

Usually standing at the eye of these hurricanes was "Red Olga," the obstreperous square-shouldered, white-haired Communist matriarch of La Victoria. Arrested in 1974 and held in the notorious Teja Verde concentration camp for two months, Olga returned to La Victoria and turned her tiny home into the "Olla Común" – the community soup kitchen that not only fed 200 families a day but served as command and control center for the local anti-Pinochet resistance.

When, during the days of the dictatorship, I found myself caught by the curfew in La Victoria, seeking the latest hard information on anything from troop movement to the price of a hamburger, or simply seeking refuge from a tear gas cloud, I would always retreat to Olga's.

But when I call her up now after not seeing her in ten years she warns, "Don't come in on the main street. You'll get robbed by the drug addicts. Come in the back way." When I finally meet up with her, she seems not to have aged. The same Yuri Gagarin picture and straw hat from Cuba hang on her dingy wall. She closed down the soup kitchen in 1990 and watched the political tide recede around her. Many of La Victoria's prob-lems are the same as they were a decade ago: high unemployment, inadequate health care, alcoholism, and a raging crack epidemic.

"The big difference now," she says, "is we no longer have any organization." The block committees, the community boards, the political rank and file groups have all but evaporated in the ether of modernity. "Now, it's everyone for himself," she sighs. "People live only for the moment. They remember nothing. They vote for anybody. We didn't have to get all the way to socialism, but we should have gotten more than this."

Olga now squeaks by on a pension of $95 a month. Her only luxury is her telephone, which eats up a fifth of her monthly income. "You try to talk to the people about changing their lives," she says. "And all they do is shrug their shoulders." As to the politicians, she has no time for them. "Funny, isn't it?" she says laughing. "After the war is over, there sure are a lot of heroes that come out of the woodwork."

A couple of miles down the smog-choked Pan-American highway and across from the plebeian Metropolitan Cemetery where I was trapped by a horrific police assault in 1983, I visit my ageing Uncle Germaín and Aunt Manuela. Their shantytown, Rio de Janeiro, couldn't have been named for anything in the Brazilian city except its infamous *favelas* – the teeming hillside slums.

Germaín and Manuela are among the bottom third of Chileans, getting by on a handful of dollars weekly. There have been changes – some for the better – since the early days of the dictatorship. Aunt Manuela's loyalties have drifted from Marx towards Jehovah, pavement now covers the dirt road in front of their shack, glass has replaced the heavy plastic in their windows, Uncle Germaín has moved from a welfare program where he swept the steps of public buildings to being a night watchman for $3 a shift, meat can be eaten two or three times a week instead of once, and a twenty-five-inch Sanyo color TV (a gift from a son) dominates their tiny sleeping quarters and seems to be permanently aglow.

But some things remain the same. None of their grandchildren can dream of paying for university, doctors' visits – even those subsidized by the tattered state healthcare system – are considered only in emergency. Medicines – indeed, the ability to stay afloat at all – would be impossible if it weren't for regular help from family living abroad. There also remains an unshakeable class-consciousness. My aunt swears blue at the mention of the military or those they protect. But old age and decades of defeat make any political response seem to her like folly.

Among Chile's bottom two-thirds of the population, the political center of gravity has shifted increasingly away from places like La Victoria and toward newer communities like La Florida. Situated at the very end of the North–South subway line, a forty-five-minute commute from downtown, composed of cracker box high-rises, cramped single-residency homes with postage-stamp-sized patios and iron fences, La Florida is an oasis for working-class and lower-middle-class families who are nowadays putting in twelve-hour workdays. La Florida's own mall, Shell station, and McDonalds sit like three sacred pyramids at the gates of the community and are a popular tourist destination for envious working-class day trippers. A decade ago, such a trio of consumerist temples could be found only in the most exclusive barrios.

Today, La Florida looms as the Chilean Dream. Scrape

together a few thousand bucks and buy your own home in the Chilean version of Levittown. No matter that you are twenty miles from the city centre, that the housing stock looks vaguely Bulgarian, that the smog and the traffic are noxious. This is all about feeling rich in miniature. This is about a concept new to Chile: Individual Lifestyle.

As I enter the living room of thirty-five-year-old Cecilia's three-bedroomed, 950-square-foot home, I feel like I need a coat of Vaseline to squeeze in. Her house, her microwave, stereo, three-year-old used car, the private school tuition for her three kids, are all leveraged on several lines of credit. Her husband makes a couple of hundred dollars a month working in a government highway toll booth.

Cecilia has been the breadwinner. She never talks about politics unless asked. But she's a staunch leftist, coming from a family of Communists and supporters of MIR – the extreme left quasi-guerrilla group pulverized by Pinochet. Until recently Cecilia was a social security saleswomen. But after three years of solid performance, she was summarily fired a few weeks previously for not having met her monthly quota of sales. "No matter how long you work for these pension agencies," she says over a cup of tea, "you can only come in under quota one month. Two months in a row and kaput."

She explains in surreal detail the corruption and unfairness of Chile's privatized social security system. Thanks to "pension reform" imposed by Pinochet in 1981, every employed and self-employed worker in Chile must contribute a percentage of his or her income every month to a private retirement fund managed by one of a half-dozen investment companies known as AFPs. Unlike the US, where both sides pay 7.5 per cent each, Chilean employers no longer make any contribution at all toward worker pensions. They retain, however, the right to withhold employee contributions from their pay checks and frequent news stories feature companies that "forget" for months and sometimes years to deposit the worker funds into the AFP. And because so many Chileans are self- or marginally employed, almost half don't actively contribute to their own funds. An equal number have been revealed to have less than a $1,000 balance – hardly enough to support retirement.

Because the fund managers invest in bonds and Chilean stocks, each fund closely mirrors the others in terms of investment choice and performance. So while there's tremendous competition among the AFPs to get as much money into its own investment pool as possible, there's little incentive for the worker to transfer from one fund to another. "That's where we salespeople come in," says Cecilia. "We work on commissions based on the new accounts we recruit. So we approach all of our friends and say give me your account and I will give you a gift. A bottle of whiskey, a cordless phone, a stereo. Right now the hot gift is a mountain bike." As a result, about half of Chilean account holders switch AFPs once every six months. About a third of those transfers, says the government, are "irregular."

"My biggest deal was a factory in Valparaiso," remembers Cecilia. "The union there pooled together thirty-four workers who offered to transfer their accounts all at once. I closed the deal. I gave the union a big-screen TV, a steam iron and a juicer which it raffled off back to the workers."

Cecilia worries little about being unemployed. She has a thriving side business representing several banks. Like an Avon lady she goes door to door in the neighborhood selling lines of credit. "All you need to show is six months' worth of pay stubs," she says. Then she can get you an immediate loan equivalent to four months' salary. Payable over twenty-four months, the interest rate is 75 per cent a year. "My father would die if he knew what I was doing. I grew up with him reading me Marx and Lenin," she says. "I still believe in all that. But I have no choice. It's sink or swim."

The same Augusto Pinochet who oversaw summary executions, whose political police tortured opponents to death and hid their bodies in pits of lye, who simply "disappeared" more than a thousand citizens, who ran scores of thousands through his jails and prisons, the same Augusto Pinochet can become Senator for Life in a few weeks because absolute impunity reigns in Chile. This results from an Amnesty Law that the military regime passed to protect itself, and is reinforced by the deal cut between the military and politicians of the Center and Left who assumed power after Pinochet's defeat in the '88 plebiscite. After the Chilean economy tanked in the early Eighties, a wave of violent protests shook the foundations of the dictatorship. The battered Left – whose electoral strength had topped out at nearly 50 per cent during the Allende period – forcefully reappeared. Along with more centrist forces they attempted to fashion the protests into massive organized civil disobedience. The most militant sectors of the opposition pushed a line of "popular rebellion" and for a brief period a low-intensity guerrilla war flickered. But by 1987, with this strategy of "rupture" still bearing no fruit, leadership of the opposition shifted to the center-right Christian Democrats (PDC), which had initially supported the Pinochet coup, only later to find themselves barred from power by the dictator. Simultaneously, Chile's largest leftist party, the Socialists – who had traditionally been on the left of the Communists – began a wholesale "renovation," moving rightward.

But by the end of the decade, confrontation with the military was supplanted by negotiation. In 1988, the civilian opposition agreed to participate in the plebiscite designed by Pinochet's regime. It was a win–win situation for the dictator. A Yes vote would give him eight more years in power. A No victory would allow him to hang on as military commander, and would allow a civilian government to be elected under the terms of his re-written constitution.

By the time of the plebiscite campaign, the Center–Left opposition, known as La Concertación, dropped any questioning of property rights and proposals for state intervention in the economy from its program. A vague call for "reconciliation" pushed justice for the military criminals off the political agenda.

The civilian opposition won the plebiscite, but that in no way ended Pinochet's model. In the months following the vote, before the first civilian election, the Christian Democrats and the Socialists held extended talks with the regime in planning the "transition." In so doing they pretty much accepted the full terms of the military. The Senate would continue to be packed with appointees, the secret police and the military would remain protected by amnesty, the archaic and pro-military judicial system would be left intact. The military budget would remain autonomous and untouchable. The new elected President would not be able to remove any top military commander for eight years. As one former army captain told me: "This was the only transition in Latin America where the military came out not only untarnished, but downright virgin." The Chilean Church, meanwhile, closed down its human rights office and turned its attention to the issues of divorce and abortion, neither of which legally exist in Chile.

The demand voiced by the thousands who celebrated in the streets on the morrow of the plebiscite that Pinochet resign from the Army, was never echoed by the civilians who a year later were elected to run the first post-Pinochet government. Pinochet became a convenient bogeyman for the new "democrats." The specter of another military coup has been a handy excuse for the Christian Democrats in maintaining as conservative a rule as possible. "How embarrassing for us," says dissident Christian Democrat Senator Jorge Lavanderos. "We could have defeated Pinochet in '83, and again in '88 but lamentably my own party negotiated away democracy with him."

The last eight years of civilian rule have been what some call a time of "excessive realism." And as the junior partners in this arrangement, the Socialist Left has moved from a position of expediency to one of complicity as co-administrator of the hemisphere's most rigidly orthodox neo-liberal system. "The Socialists now pretend to be the opposition while still staying in the government," says a leader of the small Humanist Party, which – along with the Communists – is one of the few Left groups not in the governing coalition. "They criticize all the programs they administer."

In giving legitimacy to a system designed by their enemies, the Socialists trivialize politics and generate vast cynicism. "Young people who are idealists, who had so many hopes when Pinochet lost the plebiscite, are finding out we are being betrayed, that a deal was cut over our heads," says Pablo Bussemius, twenty-five-year-old Socialist student body president at the national law school. "Now with Pinochet headed for the Senate, there's an ever greater disillusionment and withdrawal from politics."

That disillusionment gelled into measurable terms in the campaign for last December's mid-term congressional elections. When the nightly fifteen minutes of free air time for political parties came on TV, ratings plummeted. A full 20 per cent of TVs were simply switched off. This in a country where, traditionally, politics had been the main dish of dinner-table talk. No surprise. The Right ran a campaign as defenders of the poor! And the Center/Left government parties broadcast a campaign that would have tingled Dick Morris's toes. "Love Is Better in Democracy," Chileans were told as the tube flashed images of couples hugging and kissing.

One TV political talk show I saw encapsulated perfectly the bankruptcy of modern Chilean politics. As a panel of the four men running for Senator from Santiago fielded inane questions from an insipid host, tuxedoed waiters walked on to camera and served them cakes and pastries while, on the corner of the stage, two teenage girls (described by the host as "journalists") sat in skimpy mini-skirts and noted down questions called in from the audience. After a commercial break, the scene shifted to the outdoor patio of the TV studio. There the host encouraged the Socialist candidate to play ping-pong against his rival from the hard right UDI Party – a party founded by Pinochet's dreaded secret police. As torturer and tortured batted the ball between them and simultaneously answered questions from the host, what could the audience have been thinking?

When the votes came in on December 11, generalized panic set in. Not because the ruling coalition lost 5 per cent of its vote or because the hard Right displaced its more moderate allies. A full 41 per cent of the eligible electorate either didn't register to vote, abstained, defaced the ballot or left it blank. A million voters under twenty-give failed to register. Predictable results for Americans. But earth-shaking for Chileans who have been accustomed to 95 per cent and higher turn-outs. In Chile's second city of Valparaiso, the first plurality in the multi-party vote went effectively to "none of the above" – 20 per cent of the ballots were defaced. In Santiago, the extra-parliamentary Communists doubled their vote to nearly 10 per cent.

The contours of the vote reveal a discontent just beneath the surface. And not withstanding the government's reluctance to take on Pinochet, nor the hard-core 30 per cent or so of the population who in some measure or another still revere him, the other 70 per cent have a visceral hatred for the dictator. He cannot appear unprotected in public without provoking cat-calls and boos. Polls have consistently shown two-thirds or more of the population in favor of his resignation.

A courageous judge in Spain is currently hearing testimony on Pinochet for "alleged crimes against humanity," including the murder of Spanish citizens in Chile. The Chilean "democratic" government has denounced the inquiry, President Eduardo Frei has blocked an attempt by a few young Christian Democrat congressmen to go forward with their own impeachment of Pinochet, and the Chilean foreign minister has called the proposed impeachment "profoundly inconvenient." But a long list of Chilean social and cultural leaders have given their public support to the Spanish investigation.

Perhaps even more significant, a Chilean appeals judge sent shockwaves through the political establishment in mid-January when he agreed to hear a case brought by Communist Party leader Gladys Marín. Marín, whose husband was "disappeared" by the military, is trying to block Pinochet from taking his Senate seat by formally charging him with "genocide, kidnapping and illegal burying of bodies." It's the first time any Chilean court has accepted a direct charge against the dictator.

So far the much-touted reconciliation in Chile has been one-sided. The military has never been asked to atone or even apologize for its crimes. And the deep reservoirs of popular resentment against the military are rarely given public voice.

But on a recent bus commute through downtown Santiago I witnessed a moving scene. A street troubadour boarded the bus to sing for his supper. This all-too-common occurrence has driven Chilean commuters beyond boredom, so barely anybody made eye contact with the roughly dressed middle-aged singer. While most of these beggers scratch out three or four tunes before asking for money, this fellow sang only one song. "*Tu, no eres nada, ni chicha ni limonada,*" he crooned, reviving the signature song of Victor Jara, the leftist folk singer whose hands were smashed before he was killed by Pinochet's military in the weeks following the coup. "You are nothing, neither hard cider nor lemonade. Get out of the middle of the road, join up and save your dignity . . ." Two or three young people clapped their Walkman earphones on as soon as he strummed his first chord. The thirty or so others on the packed bus listened quietly as they stared ahead or out of the window. But when he finished, almost everyone put coins in his cup.

A stroll through downtown Santiago provides a reminder of how mesmerizing and paralyzing mass consumer culture is when newborn. In America, consumerism sprang as a natural outgrowth of booming economic development, but in Chile, mass credit consumerism substitutes for development. Worse, before 1973, conspicuous consumption was taboo in a country still infused with a sense of social solidarity. Television didn't arrive here until 1962. There were no malls until the early Eighties. No fast food till a few years later.

Imagine, the *frisson* the average Chilean feels today when he or she walks the Alameda, the main downtown thoroughfare, and sees all the world's baubles offered up for sale and on easy credit. At the entrance to every department store, every shoe store, every pharmacy, there is the ubiquitous young girl manning a podium offering instant credit. Air Nikes? Cash price 29,000 *pesos*. Or twelve payments of 2,900 *pesos*. A bottle of Shalimar? Cash price 16,000 *pesos*. Or ten payments of 2,200 *pesos*. That is ten monthly payments of five dollars each.

Radical sociologist Tomás Moulian points to a massifying of credit as only the latest step in implementing a neo-liberal economic model a quarter-century in the making. In one of Chile's sweetest ironies, his book on the subject, *The Real Chile: Anatomy of a Myth,* stayed on the domestic bestseller list through all of 1997.

"What we have in Chile," he says "is the marriage of a neo-liberal economy with a neo-democracy, a simulated democracy. The end result is a neo-liberal system now defended by its historic adversaries. Pinochet, for his part, is a symbol of this capitalist counter-revolution which profoundly changed our culture and even the capitalism we had before him."

Moulian's thesis runs something like this: The first two years of military rule merely reversed the Allende era reforms, liberalized prices, lowered salaries and subjected the working class to the now familiar nostrums of economic "shock therapy." The Chicago Boys period of 1975–82, shaped by Milton Friedman and Ted Harbeger, introduced structural reforms, increased exports, and created new economic groups indebted to international banks. A draconian labor law clamped down on workers, and a wave of privatization, including social security pensions, atrophied the state. That phase fizzled out in 1983 in a mini-depression that liquidated national industry and drove half the population below the subsistence poverty level.

"But a sense of direction was recovered immediately," says Moulian. "A re-ordering, a re-privatization of everything commenced under a neo-liberal pattern. The new economic groups that emerged were much stronger than the older ones. Not indebted to foreign capital, they were interwoven with it. And the tremendous pools of private money generated by the private pension funds were used to fuel these new groups. It was the workers' money that built such prosperity for the elite. This Chilean model," continues Moulian, "anticipates Reagan and Thatcher. Owing to the neo-liberal intellectual sway over the military, Chile started out early on the road that everybody is now on."

Adds Moulian: "In this sense the Chilean terror was rational. This whole model is frankly impossible without a dictatorship. Only the dictatorship could have disciplined the working class into submission while their salaries were lowered and their pensions used to accumulate wealth for others. Only a dictatorship can keep a country quiet while education, universities, and healthcare are privatized, and while an absolute marketization of the labor force is imposed. Today, under this simulated democracy, the work force is too fragmented to recover and the population is distracted by consumerism and disciplined by credit obligations."

Drive around the "Little Manhattan" section of Santiago's Barrio Alto – its lavish "High Neighborhood" – and you'll come face to face with the few who are perched atop the steep pyramid of Chilean social class. Fifty per cent of all new national construction in the last decade has taken place in just two wealthy suburbs: Vitacura and Las Condes. In the hillside neighborhood of La Dehesa the family house that is a replica of Tara pales beside the reproduction of Versailles. It seems there are only two types of vehicle up here – Mercedes sedans and the shuttle buses that cart domestic help to and from the shanty-towns – the same sort of shuttles that scurry between Soweto and the Johannesburg suburb of Bird Haven.

A little closer to downtown but only a half notch down the social scale, the municipality of Providencia is a delight of lush gardens and colonial mansions. Its City Hall is a converted Tuscan villa replete with marble columns, stained glass and crystal chandeliers. Its manicured rose garden is a favorite meeting place for uniformed nannies taking their stroller-bound charges for an afternoon airing.

I've come to meet the elected Mayor of Providencia, former army colonel Cristian Lebbé. I knew his father, who was also a colonel until Allende sacked him after he refused to salute Fidel Castro visiting back in 1971. The young Labbé followed his dad's footsteps into the military and Pinochet became his mentor. From the dictator's security apparatus, Labbé became one of his trusted political advisers, eventually serving as Chief Minister of Government in the last two years of the regime.

Outfitted in a white shirt and two Mont Blanc pens in his pocket, his blond hair greased straight back in the preferred style of the Chilean aristocracy, Labbé receives me with tea in his personal office. There is a tangible diffidence in his manner. Not because of my association with Allende, of which I deliberately do not inform him, but because, of all things, I am an American. In the bizarre ideological universe of extreme nationalism and creeping neo-Nazism that Labbé inhabits, Americans are viewed as busybody socialists. He tells me right off that he's still angry over the pressure the US exerted on

Pinochet to stage his 1988 plebiscite. "We carried out each one of our promises even though no one believed us," Labbé says with a red face. "Not even you gringos believed us. We had every organ of the US government down here acting as if they owned us."

I let the remark pass and ask him to reflect on Pinochet's legacy. "We live in a democracy today only because of the work of the military government," he fires back. "Chileans today recognize the morality of merit and incentives. Chileans know that if you want to – you can. Today, if you do well, you are respected, not scorned. A Mercedes today is a symbol of success. Now we have freedom of choice, as Milton Friedman says. Man is free to buy or not to buy. Once we had two universities. Now we have 300. Once we had one type of car. Now there are twenty or thirty. That is freedom."

When I ask about the social cost of such liberation, about a certain legacy of human rights abuse, Labbé cuts me off with a condescending smile. "There's a terrible auto accident. The victim has no vital signs and is barely breathing. He's rushed to the emergency room and his whole family begins *demanding* everything and anything be done to save him. The surgeons start cutting and operating. The patient revives slowly. First he goes to urgent care. Then he's put on a strict diet. Some of his activities are also restricted. With careful treatment over years he fully recuperates. He's even free to choose another doctor if he wants. And one day he goes to the beach. When he takes his shirt off, his brother sees a bunch of scars and stitch marks. And the brother is scandalized! Shocked! 'My God,' he says, 'you are a victim of human rights abuses.'"

At least Labbé, in his roundabout way, recognizes the scars. That's more than a lot of his constituents will do. I know, because some of these Chilean holocaust deniers are in my own family. After tea with the colonel I walk a few blocks to my fifty-something cousin Sonia's gate-guarded Providencia apartment. I dine with her and a thirty-five-year-old third cousin, Lisette, the fair-skinned daughter of a wealthy businessman. Both women are what is called in popular lingo *momias*, reactionary mummies. But even I wasn't prepared for the dialogue that ensued.

"What a catastrophe these last eight years of [civilian] government have been," said Sonia. "We are back to strikes, disorder, corruption. Pinochet was grand. He brought order and depoliticized the country."

I answer: "Well, he also is responsible for killing and torturing a lot of people."

"Outside of Chile that's what they say happened," interrupts Lisette. "But it's not true. I've always said if you weren't doing anything wrong, nothing would happen to you. Nothing happened to me. I never saw anyone killed. Though I will say this, these eight years haven't been as bad as I thought they were going to be. Democracy isn't as bad as everyone predicted."

I press on with the subject of death and disappearance, raising the murder of Orlando Letelier by Chilean secret police in Washington DC, the bombing murder of former General Carlos Prats in Buenos Aires, the 3,192 dead listed by the government-named Truth Commission, and finally my own experience of narrowly escaping Chile a week after the coup and the fact that so many of their own family members including my wife were forced into exile.

"I don't know about this or that fact," answers Sonia, totally unfazed. "All I know is what I have lived through personally. And personally I was much happier, I felt much safer with Pinochet."

And there you have the psychological cost of impunity. It's what Tomás Moulian calls "the great psychotic denial." When there's never been an acknowledgement from the armed forces of any wrongdoing, when the civilian government including the Socialists demand no such recognition, when the Right and Left trumpet Chile as the model of the future, when the dictator remains free to become Senator, when torturers and assassins are exempted from prosecution, then anything said to the contrary must be a lie. To admit otherwise would be to acknowledge at what horrible price come the privileges of Providencia.

The Chilean military can no longer afford to live in the economy they created. During the dictatorship they took on huge mortgages and big car payments and now, removed from direct power, they are struggling to pay the bills in a rampant free market economy. "They are very worried," says long-time military affairs expert, writer Raúl Sohr. "The military is the child of the state. And to the state they have returned. While the rest of the country has to put up with privatized everything, the military now has its own schools, its own hospitals, its own vacation camps, its own subsidized housing, transportation, and

universities. It even has its own state pensions. They have their
own private socialism."

Beyond the irony of this anecdote, there's also a caveat about
Chile's future. Chilean soldiers aren't the only citizens poised on
the economic razor's edge. The country's economic stability is
leveraged on continuing exports and expanding consumer
credit – two pillars easily knocked out by fluctuations in the
world market. Already, the Asian economic crisis has caused the
Chilean stock market dive this year and an unprecedented but to
date still controllable dip in the peso. The last time the Chilean
economy took a tumble, in 1983, the country went to the brink
of rebellion – and that was under the heel of military rule.

"The greatest enemy to future stability is a sort of generalized ignorance and arrogance that comes with triumphalism,"
says Ricardo Israel, Director of the University of Chile's Political
Sciences Institute. "People are satisfied, saying we now have the
same products you can buy in New York or London. We are also
laden with the tremendous ideological weight of the Church
and the armed forces. We are still way behind in Chile. Yet so
many Chileans have deluded themselves into thinking we are
the vanguard. Hardly. Maybe a vanguard in duty-free shops.
Nothing more."

There's also a growing social restlessness and effervescence
in the context of a political system that generates no political
legitimacy. In spite of the fragmentation imposed over the last
twenty-five years, many Chileans remain passionate about politics but find no institutional channel for expression.

There have been some intriguing symptoms of this recently.
The eviscerated labor movement has finally started to distance

itself from its "partners" in government. Last October, 80,000 young people jammed the National Stadium – one of the dictatorship's infamous killing fields – for a concert to commemorate the thirtieth anniversary of Che Guevara's death. The extra-parliamentary Left won student body elections in two of the country's three main universities. And when in November it won in the third, the fiercely conservative Catholic University, the shockwaves battered both the Right and the official pro-government Left. "When the children of the elite vote for the hard Left, you better believe something is happening," says Raúl Sohr. Says Colonel Labbé: "I tell you I just can't understand it. Why would the students of La Católica vote Communist?"

Augusto Pinochet is celebrating his eighty-second birthday the evening I leave Chile. His morning starts with civilian supporters lining the sidewalks in front of his Barrio Alto mansion to applaud him. Then come the official visits of the entire army brass. With what the newspapers called a "visibly emotional" Pinochet looking on from his balcony, the official army band serenades him. Then the General and future Senator for Life requests a rendition of the "Erika" march followed up by his favorite tune, "Lilli Marlene."

An editorial by Cristian Labbé lauding "the vision of statesman Pinochet" appears in the leading daily, *El Mercurio* (a former beneficiary of CIA funding).

At twelve noon, a couple of dozen anti-Pinochet student leaders gather in front of the downtown Defense Ministry and unfurl a banner offering the General a one-way ticket to Spain for his birthday. Seconds later, squads of national police attack the students and several journalists, clubbing them, tear-gassing them and arresting them. No one knows under what charges. And no one asks.

By 8pm Pinochet has arrived at the army's so-called Rock House where he is fêted by 1,300 guests including several top industrialists, army officers, TV personalities, and the former Chilean Miss Universe. The President Pinochet Foundation is transmitting the event by closed circuit to thirty-six other banquets in Pinochet's honor across the country. Three of Chile's private TV networks are also transmitting the entire event. As I head to the airport I hear Pinochet's crackly voice over the radio telling his supporters that he is "perfectly aware" of the "destructive ambitions" harbored by those who criticize the military. "Anything that affects any single member of the Army," he warns, "affects the whole Army."

When my taxi crosses into downtown we are snarled in traffic. Some 5,000 mostly young protestors are in the streets blocking traffic, singing and wishing the General a "very unhappy birthday and all the sorrow in the world." To make my flight I have to dodge the water cannons, the barricades, the bonfires, and tear-gas. But I do so with pleasure. This evening Chile seems more like the country I knew twenty-five years ago. This demonstration is very different from the skirmishes staged all month by the social security sales force. These students are fighting for much more than their narrow personal interests. You hope they are not the last rattle of the snake of rebellion and liberation. You hope that, against the odds, they will help millions of others remember a future.

RESURRECTION: ADIOS, GENERAL!

DECEMBER 1999–SEPTEMBER 2000

When Augusto Pinochet arrived in London in late September 1998, he couldn't have imagined that he might never see Chile again. Even less that he might wind up seeing the inside of a prison cell. Pinochet had been a regular visitor to the United Kingdom whenever he fancied shopping at Harrods or dropping in for tea with Baroness Thatcher. On occasion he would also take time out to conduct arms purchases from British defense merchants.

But this visit by the eighty-two-year-old former dictator was different. It was primarily for medical reasons – back trouble and complications from diabetes. There was also a PR aspect to Pinochet's London sojourn. An attempt was being made to tidy up his image, and so the former dictator allowed a reporter from the *New Yorker* an unusually lengthy interview.

Pinochet then underwent back surgery and took up convalescence in the posh and private London Clinic. The plan was to rest up and head back home where he would exercise his new position as a Chilean Senator for Life. I am not the first to point out the irony of the General's chosen facility of convalescence. Santiago also had its own London Clinic – La Clínica Londres. This latter facility, however, was run by Pinochet's secret police, the CNI, and its patients were more likely to be connected to high-voltage electrodes than any life-saving equipment.

Pinochet's earlier visits to Britain had been low-profile, often secret. And so the publicity that accompanied this last visit of Pinochet to London is something the dictator will regret for however many years he has left alive. Indeed, on October 15 1998, the fine London daily the *Guardian* published a provocative column by veteran Latin American correspondent Hugh O'Shaughnessy about the General's presence in the country. Under the inflammatory title of "A Murderer Among Us," the column called for the arrest of Pinochet for his various crimes against humanity.

It is unlikely that O'Shaughnessy thought his call would materialize in fact.

But in Spain, a dashing and indomitable judge by the name of Baltazar Garzón had also learned of Pinochet's presence in London and had decided it was time to try and nab his prey. For two years Garzón and another Spanish magistrate had been investigating the deaths of several Spanish citizens in Chile and Argentina. Atop the pyramid of murder and torture uncovered by their investigation sat none other than Augusto Pinochet.

And so it was that around the time the *Guardian* column appeared in print, the Spanish legal authorities contacted Interpol and a Red Notice warrant was issued for the arrest of the Chilean dictator. Late on the night of October 16 1998, two plain-clothes agents of London's Metropolitan Police entered the private clinic where Pinochet was asleep. They disarmed and sent home his two Chilean bodyguards.

Rousing the General from his medicated sleep, the police informed Pinochet that he was now under arrest on various counts of murder, torture, genocide, and conspiracy. Armed police were posted at the doors of the Clinic: the convalescing Pinochet was officially in British custody awaiting extradition for trial in Spain.

Baltazar Garzón, the man who engineered Pinochet's arrest, had already obtained a reputation in Spain as a fearless "super-judge," taking on the same national administrations that had promoted him as a magistrate, when, in 1996, he began to focus on Latin America. He was looking into the cases of more than 300 Spanish citizens who had been caught up in the "dirty war" of mass killing by the Argentine military dictatorship of the 1970s. His investigation led him right into the middle of Operation Condor – the network of intelligence services and cross-border murder concocted by Pinochet's Chile, the generals of Argentina and other neighboring Latin American dictatorships.

In these endeavours he soon came across the diligent work of another Spaniard, Juan Garcés. A former aide to and confidant of Salvador Allende, Garcés had been by the Chilean President's side inside the Moneda Palace on the day of the coup. After returning to Spain, Garcés continued to champion the dead President's cause and wrote several books on Chile that damned the Pinochet regime.

But Garcés also worked tirelessly to compile files of evidence showing the hand of Pinochet and his military regime in the killing, disappearance, and torture of several Spanish citizens. He eventually shared those files with Garzón, who was able to use the quirks of Spanish law to do what no Chilean court had ever dared – to order the arrest of General Pinochet himself.

The news of Pinochet's arrest exploded around the globe. Overnight, a new benchmark in international law was achieved. No longer would human rights criminals be free to roam the globe after formally leaving whatever posts – including head of state – they held in their national governments.

In Chile, the arrest shook the foundations of society like a political earthquake. The bagging of Pinochet rudely punctured the bubble of legal impunity that the dictator granted himself and his collaborators with a 1978 "amnesty" decree. It has also highlighted the stomach-turning cowardice of Chile's nominally Center-Left civilian government which sprung to Pinochet's defense, grotesquely arguing that El Senador be shielded by diplomatic immunity. Chilean President Eduardo Frei, in apparent refutation of the Nuremberg principles, proclaimed: "Chileans should be judged only by Chilean courts." But Socialist congressman Juan Pablo Letelier – whose father Orlando was killed in a 1976 Washington DC car bomb set by Pinochet's secret police – answered by saying "immunity does not equal impunity," meaning that the formal amnesty self-granted by Pinochet should no longer be seen as a shield against prosecution.

For the next year, legal sparring over Pinochet pinballed throughout the British legal system. On the one side, Pinochet's private lawyers ran through a gamut of defenses from diplomatic immunity to national sovereignty in an attempt to free the General. In these efforts they continued to be aided by the Chilean government – the putatively anti-Pinochet elected government – that seemed desperate to avoid the General standing trial.

On the other side, international human rights groups filed auxiliary briefs demanding that Pinochet face justice. And within weeks, more than a half-dozen other European governments also demanded Pinochet's extradition for the murder of their own citizens.

The Pinochet case took several sharp and surprising turns. But more than a year after his capture, Pinochet was still in custody. The House of Lords, the British equivalent of the Supreme Court, had narrowed the charges down to acts of torture committed after 1988 – the year the UK signed an international treaty against such acts. But the bottom line was the same: until or unless some other legal appeal could undo things, Pinochet was headed towards a Spanish courtroom.

It was against that background that I once again returned to Chile in December 1999, fourteen months into Pinochet's custody, and my first time in a Chile free of Pinochet.

It is a balmy December evening in this southern hemisphere spring, and nearly a quarter of a million people jam the narrow concrete canyon of Santiago's main thoroughfare – La

Alameda. I am enveloped in a mammoth, pulsing, closing campaign event of Socialist Ricardo Lagos – the heavily favored presidential candidate of Chile's ruling coalition. And, for me, this night crackles with special memory. The stage Lagos is to speak from is just a few steps away from my old apartment in the San Borja complex. The flapping flags, the pounding music, the heat of the crowd as it chants, dances, and cheers all seem lifted from those days in the early Seventies when I could watch from my seventeenth-floor living-room window equal and sometimes greater numbers of Chileans rally in these same streets around President Allende.

I am exhilarated to return to Chile during this election campaign. Standing in the middle of this Santiago election rally on the eve of the millennium is positively electrifying. I was now returning to a Chile cleansed for the first time of Pinochet's physical presence.

Pinochet's arrest, eight months after he donned his senatorial sash, came just at the moment when Chile appeared on the verge of having its collective memory erased for ever. The aftershocks are still being felt here more than a year after the fact.

"When he was arrested it was like a lightning bolt," says human rights attorney Fabiola Letelier, the aunt of Juan Pablo and sister of the assassinated Orlando, whom I see just before going off to the Lagos campaign rally. "Something like 70 per cent of us Chileans felt with that arrest that justice could at least be achieved somewhere – if not in Chile. In the year or so since then, this country has not been the same."

The changes are dramatic. After nearly disappearing from

public debate, Chile's unresolved human rights history has been unceremoniously thrust front and center. Some of the guilty, those who fearlessly strutted the boulevards only a few months ago, are now being brought to justice. As the Chilean justice system begins to recover some of its independence, a half-dozen generals – intimates and close allies of Pinochet – and dozens of other former military officers are being indicted for their bloodletting. More than fifty cases have been lodged against Pinochet himself in Chilean courts.

Under pressure from human rights groups and led by the diligence of the non-profit National Security Archives in Washington DC, the American government has begun to declassify thousands of its heretofore secret documents on Chile and Pinochet. New details are being learned about the long, bloody reach of Operation Condor and its victims. And some of those documents show that the CIA may have given the Pinochet regime the green light to murder my two American friends who perished in the first days of the dictatorship, Charlie Horman and Frank Teruggi. Human rights cases stemming from Pinochet's regime that have lain dormant are now being re-activated from Washington to Brussels to Berne.

In Santiago, bookshelves now display new volumes on Allende's virtues and Pinochet's crimes. A courageous group called La Funa is "outing" unpunished torturers. The military draft and the Army's secret budget are publicly challenged. Endemic police brutality is reported and scrutinized.

After nearly succumbing to the twin ills of enforced collective amnesia and the bewildering glitter of a new credit-driven consumerist culture, the other Chile that shined in the early

Seventies – the Chile of compassion, solidarity, and social justice – struggles to be reborn. But it does so against steep odds.

"This past year has been fantastic," says veteran human rights lawyer fifty-two-year-old Hector Salazar who has recently been successful in getting some top former army generals arrested and into court. "Everyone is finally starting to recognize that human rights is *the* issue that now has to be resolved," he continues. "What is absolutely incredible is that the election campaign now under way in Chile has barely mentioned this issue, that the political structure of Chile now pretends General Pinochet never existed."

Absolutely incredible is, perhaps, an understatement.

In his gripping and final broadcast speech while the Moneda Presidential Palace was under air and ground attack by Pinochet, and just moments before he killed himself, Salvador Allende had boldly predicted that one day, "sooner rather than later," free Chileans would once again stroll the central boulevard of the Alameda.

Tonight, on that same boulevard, in the visceral stir of the Ricardo Lagos campaign rally, it is seductive to believe that that moment has finally come. Pinochet is out of Chile, out of the Senate, and in British custody. His legacy is in tatters. His collaborators are under judicial heat. And for the first time since Allende's history-making election in 1970, a Socialist Party candidate – Ricardo Lagos – is favored to take the presidency.

And yet, just at the moment when it seems conditions are ripe to give Pinochet the final boot into history's trash can, just when it appears possible to heal Chile's gaping wounds, General Pinochet has suddenly disappeared as completely from the official political debate as any one of his previous victims did from his or her home. The man who single-handedly dominated Chilean politics for two and a half decades has been effectively kidnapped and hustled off the scene by a conspiracy of the entire Chilean political establishment.

Why the political Right and its presidential candidate, Joaquin Lavín – who just the previous year were staging noisy street marches demanding the dictator's return – would bury Pinochet is a no-brainer. The totality of the Right had always publically venerated Pinochet and sworn eternal loyalty. But who wants to go into a national presidential election trumpeting the legacy of a leader who was now an indicted international war criminal? Though they would never admit it, the more enlightened among Chile's right-wing politicians were secretly delighted to be able to jettison their disgraced and decrepit General and take a tentative step toward political modernity.

But how to explain the Center-Left government and its Socialist candidate Lagos' punting on Pinochet? At first blush it would seem absurd. But is was wholly predictable. No sooner had Pinochet been arrested in October 1997, than the government coalition – known as the Concertación and forged in the anti-Pinochet plebiscite of a decade earlier – began demanding the dictator's liberation. Clearly figuring that it would be politically more advantageous to please Chile's right-wing economic elite than to follow through on promises of social justice, the government coalition of centrist Christian Democrats and equally moderate Socialists has not wavered in its call to short-circuit any trial for Pinochet.

Worse, it's an open secret to most Chileans just what sort of "non-aggression pact" had been negotiated between the rival Lagos and Lavín campaigns. Though Lavín, the Mayor of Chile's richest enclave Las Condes, had been a Pinochet advisor and propagandist, Lagos would not link the two men. In return, Lavín would not hammer at Lagos having once been appointed to a diplomatic post by Allende. The past, though unresolved and still deeply dividing Chile, would simply be ignored.

"The government has squandered an historic opportunity," is the way policy analyst Tim Frasca puts it. Frasca, an American who has lived in Chile for sixteen years, is the executive director of Chile's leading anti-AIDS institution. "This is like a boxing match where one side possesses the knock-out punch but won't use it. Once Pinochet was finally down, the government could have rallied the country to get beyond the current paralysis once and for all and move toward the reforms it once promised. Instead, it just rolled over."

When asked about Pinochet, candidate Lagos has repeatedly promised, if elected, to continue the policy of current President Eduardo Frei: to demand that the United Kingdom stop his extradition process to Spain and return the dictator to Chile for "humanitarian reasons."

So there is little surprise that at the Lagos rally on the Alameda, the folk group on stage has dusted off a rousing version of the anti-dictatorship anthem, "Adios General!": but the General's name, his legacy, his future, are never mentioned by Lagos or anyone else on stage.

Indeed, this is not a rally of a movement out to change the world, or even to change Chile very much. It's a modern political TV event, driven by soap star MCs and *Star Wars* soundtracks draped in the populist clothing of a more traditional Chile.

Lagos first emerged in the 1980s as a leader of the political opposition to Pinochet. He rocketed to prominence back in 1988 when he appeared on Chilean TV in a political debate and wagged a recriminating finger at a then all-powerful Dictator Pinochet. But Lagos' radical fires – and those of his Socialist Party, my party when I worked for Allende – have long been extinguished. His campaign slogan, "Growth With Equity," tells the whole somnolent story. For the past decade of civilian rule, the Socialists have been the junior partners in two successive lackluster Christian Democratic administrations. Now the Christian Democrats are pledged to support Lagos.

At his campaign rally, Lagos – who held various cabinet posts through the Nineties – hits his highest moral note by saying that the coming election between him and Lavín is, in reality, a choice "between a Chile in which people are worth only what they possess, or are worth who they really are."

A nice thought. But an empty one to those who have experienced the disappointments of the last ten years of post-Pinochet government and have recognized Lagos and his allies as no more than managers of a system put in place by the dictator.

Hector Salazar, who says he is voting for Lagos as the lesser of two evils, expresses a deep bitterness with his candidate. As a member of Lagos' campaign advisory team, Salazar says all of his suggestions on how to turn Pinochet's arrest into a catalyst for resolving so much of Chile's unfinished human rights issues were simply ignored by Lagos. There are only two explanations for the government's refusal to tackle Pinochet directly, says Salazar. It's either "a private agreement to protect Pinochet and his family in return for his leaving power ten years ago" or, more likely, it's what has become all too obvious over the last decade: the governing elite has entwined itself even more closely with Chile's ultra-conservative military and business establishments and doesn't want to rock the boat. Says Salazar: "How else to explain such softness?"

The government's most popular figure, Minister of Justice Soledad Alvear, makes no excuses for her administration's record on human rights. I meet with her the morning after Lagos' street rally and just three days before she is to resign her post to take command of Lagos' turbulent presidential campaign. "We have had our problems," the minister says. "But overall I think the Chilean transition has been exemplary." As we talk of human rights, she downplays the significance of Pinochet's arrest and suggests that, prior to it, Chile was already well on its way to prosecuting numerous human rights abuses – a plain distortion of reality. As to Pinochet's future and his possible trial in Spain, she repeats the now well-known government line: "All I can say is that it is we Chileans who should be the only ones to judge whatever happened here in Chile."

At that moment I can't help but smile, remembering what professor and author Saul Landau told me in Los Angeles shortly before I boarded the plan to Chile. Since the 1976

murder of his friend Orlando Letelier, Landau has worked tirelessly behind the scenes to bring Pinochet to justice. "Marc,
when they tell you in Chile that Pinochet should be tried in
Chile," he said laughing cynically, "remember to ask them to
show you the arrest warrant and indictment."

Carmen Soria, thirty-nine, who sits with me at a downtown
Santiago café, scoffs when I repeat Alvear's words. "Look," she
says, "the government position on Pinochet is the same as the
Pinochetistas'. It's just radically more hypocritical." Soria's
relentless and fearless pursuit for justice in Chile led one magazine to dub her the "Woman Who Makes the Army Tremble."
And rightly so. Indeed, General Pinochet's eventual arrest in
Europe can, in part, be traced back to Soria, who now hosts a
daily radio show on a low-power university transmitter.

It was in June 1976 that her father, Carmelo, a leftist
Spanish refugee and a functionary at a UN office in Satiago,
was kidnapped by the so-called Mulchen Brigade of Pinochet's
feared secret police. Over a two-day period Soria, was tortured
to death.

In 1990 Carmen and other surviving relatives brought his
case to the Chilean courts. "But as expected," Carmen says,
"the case was eventually thrown out because of the Amnesty
Law. The government then tried to make a deal with me," she
continues. "They offered me a statue to my father and a million
dollars in a settlement." In a public letter in 1997 Soria
squashed the offer. "I looked them in the eye and told them: 'I
don't forget treason. You might feel comfortable paying the

salaries of this government with the blood of those who died. But don't make me complicit with you.'" Instead, Soria's request before the Inter-American Court of the Organization of American States to open a case against the Chilean government for "denial of justice" was granted in late 1999.

But Carmelo Soria's case, as championed by his daughter, has already had international reverberations. The murder of her father was one of the foundations of the legal thrust made against Pinochet in Spain by Judge Garzón and Juan Garcés. Finally, thanks to their tireless work, the stunning arrest of Pinochet and the domino-like fall of so many other military officers this past year, the carefully erected stone wall of Chilean impunity was being breached.

But it isn't the only fissure. After two decades of quiet obeisance to the dictatorship, even after it had left power, the Chilean justice system has started to recover at least a small quota of its surrendered dignity. Magistrate Juan Guzman Tapia has opened more than fifty murder cases against Pinochet – almost all of them since the General's arrest – and is currently seeking to interrogate the former dictator.

Guzman Tapia and another Chilean judge have also found a novel way to pierce the shield of the Amnesty Law enacted by the dictatorship before it left power. Because the bodies of the "disappeared" have never been found, the two judges have ruled that these cases are "perpetual kidnappings." These crimes may have commenced before the 1978 cut-off date for the amnesty but they are still ongoing in the present because the fate of the missing is not known. And other high-profile acts of state terrorism committed after 1978 are now under active prosecution.

The result? What the current Chilean army chief called, with evident disgust, a "parade of military officers and police" before the courts of justice. Six generals, including two former chiefs of the secret police, as well as four dozen other former high-ranking officers, have found themselves indicted in the last few months. Just before New Year, former Air Force General Fernando Matthei, a former member of the dictatorship's ruling junta, was interrogated by a magistrate investigating the execution of two dissidents.

"We've been going into the courts since 1973 and kept banging our heads against the Amnesty Law," says Fabiola Letelier in her cramped office, a portrait of her murdered brother Orlando peering over her shoulder. Like Carmen Soria, the outspoken Letelier has a police bodyguard. "So there's a warehouse of information on record that is now coming into play. I'm optimistic finally that more and more cases will now go ahead and that proper sentences will be gotten. But let's be clear: this is a result of *international* justice and *international* pressure. That's what's created this opening."

Letelier and other human rights activists are encouraged, arguing that as increasing numbers of officers fall, more will talk to save their skins. The current flurry of open cases could easily snowball. Defenders of the dictatorship have consequently reacted with horror to the sudden outbreak of justice. Earlier this year, right-wing Senator Herman Larraín told a local reporter: "Amnesty comes from the Greek word amnesia and means to forget the existence of something. These cases should not be analyzed or researched."

The Chilean government has also displayed fears that the lid of silence might be inconveniently blown off to unleash two decades of pent-up demand for justice. So it was back in August that the civilian Minister of Defense proposed the creation of a so-called Dialogue Roundtable between the military and human rights groups. The military – which to date has recognized no human rights problem under its dictatorship – clearly wanted to cut its potential losses in courts and accepted the offer. While Chilean human rights groups – like the Group of Families of the Disappeared – were pleased to see the military on the defensive, they refused to formally enter the talks, arguing that the military was looking to bargain its way out of assuming its historic guilt.

A number of individual human rights lawyers – including Hector Salazar – nevertheless agreed to participate in the talks with the armed forces. About a dozen inconclusive Roundtable meetings have taken place. "The military has a lot to lose and nothing to win," says Salazar. "Sooner or later they have to accept responsibility for what they did. Essentially, they want to trade bones for certain impunity. We are not going to accept that."

Fabiola Letelier's CODEPU group is among those opposing the Roundtable: "We rejected it right away," she says, flipping through a sheaf of press releases against it. "It's part of a government strategy aimed at showing that Chile can settle at a table what it refuses to settle in the courts. They are going to try and shut us up by offering up some missing bones. But bones are only the 'archaeological truth.' There's much, much more at play than just bones. There's our whole denied history."

All this renewed human rights activity is unfolding against the Lagos–Lavín presidential contest which refuses even to address the issue. That reality, combined with the government's extraordinary call to free Pinochet, has so disillusioned activists like Carmen Soria that she says it matters very little if the governing Concertación wins a third term or if the Pinochetistas behind Lavín return to power. "I don't want Lavín to win," says Soria. "But on the other hand, if he comes to power it might be for the best. Let the Concertación go into opposition and break apart, so finally a real social movement can emerge here. The student and labor movements are now being led by the Left. It's about time we finally came out and fought for change and justice. Everyone has been too quiet the last ten years."

Election night, Sunday December 12 1999, and the Chilean government counts the vote with Swiss precision and velocity. A political upset is under way. The early count is denying Ricardo Lagos – among six candidates – the easy first-round victory confidently predicted by his campaign. It's clear by 7pm that, falling short of 50 per cent, Lagos will be forced into a second round. By 8pm, the tally of right-wing candidate Lavín is surprisingly high. Numerous polls had suggested Lavín would finish strongly enough to force a run-off but few foresaw Lavín coming close to victory. By 10.30 the final count is in. Not only is a run-off required to decide the presidency a month hence but Lavín has stood the Chilean political life on its head by scoring a virtual tie. Lagos finishes with 47.9 per cent, 10 per cent less than the governing coalition won in the last presidential election. Lavín bags 47.5 per cent, 10 per cent more than the traditional conservative vote.

Many theories are offered as to why, just at the moment when Pinochet is under indictment and his legacy lies in ruins, his political heirs and allies are threatening to win the presidency. The most logical explanation is that it is the inevitable product of a situation where the anti-Pinochet forces have become the managers and defenders of the system the dictator designed, while the pro-Pinochet forces now pose as its populist critics.

Or, as historian Alfredo Jocelyn-Holt put it on the eve of the voting: "However the elections results turn out, the [government] Concertación is mortally wounded because it has already fulfilled its role as 'legitimator' of the institutional plans of the dictatorship drawn up in 1977."

Meanwhile, the posh Crowne Plaza Hotel, which has served as Lavín's campaign headquarters, brims with election-night euphoria. Chile's best and brightest, its blond and beautiful, its creamy elite has gathered together to celebrate its unexpected victory at the polls. In a corner of one of the rented banquet rooms I meet up with four teenage supporters of Lavín – all of them from the wealthy enclave of Vitacura. One of them, seventeen-year-old Antonia de La Maza, is the daughter of Lavín's campaign manager. There ensues once again one of those brain-boggling conversations of which I have had too many in my years of contact with Chile. As I write their words in my notebook, I remember my bizarre conversation two years earlier with my Aunt Sonia – an expert at living in political denial. The teenagers fire off their one-liners with staccato speed:

"Pinochet wasn't a dictator. Pinochet freed our country from Communism. He is a hero."

"Chile has been defamed by the international press."

"Not as many people died as they say. The Communists fabricated the death toll."

"Most of the people who died were soldiers killed by terrorists."

"No one was ever tortured in Chile. That's a lie."

The only boy among this group, nineteen-year-old Francisco del Piero, goes the farthest in conceding any atrocities. "The error the military made was not giving back the bodies," he says. "The killings were OK. But they should have returned the bodies."

I leave the hotel and head for the street at midnight thinking that this chilling conversation is the price Chile paid for not passing through a process of de-Nazification. Now there's a new, second generation of Chileans living in denial. For when there's never been an apology or even a recognition from the armed forces of any crimes, when the following elected government – including the Socialists – demands no such gesture, when the same government calls for the liberation of the dictator who was at the center of the killing, and when murderers sit as appointed senators in the national congress, then, it would seem, no one is in fact guilty.

Call it a supreme irony. A month later on January 16 2000, in second-round voting, Socialist Ricardo Lagos won the presidency, defeating Lavín by a 51–48 per cent margin. And he seems to have been boosted over the top by none other than Pinochet himself.

Just a handful of days before the ballot, British Home Secretary Jack Straw announced he was "minded" to send Pinochet back to Chile on "humanitarian" grounds. Straw claimed that a medical exam, whose results remained secret, revealed the old dictator to be unfit to stand trial in Spain.

In Chile, the news of Pinochet's imminent return burst into the headlines. What Lagos had refused to do was now being accomplished indirectly by the media. Potential voters were being starkly reminded that rival candidate Lavín had been an apologist for the war criminal now being sent back home.

The good news for Lagos was that he had won. The bad news was that his bluff about Pinochet standing trial in Chile was being called. For all his efforts to bury the Pinochet controversy, here it was once again erupting front and center.

As the election results confirmed his victory, President-elect Ricardo Lagos appeared before a roiling crowd of 60,000 to deliver his victory speech. He struggled to evoke his vision of economic growth for the future. But thousands in the crowd ignored his words and repeatedly chanted "Put Pinochet On Trial!" He quieted down the crowd only to have them once again loudly demand that the dictator be tried if returned to Chile.

Human rights lawyers announced they were preparing to strip Pinochet of his parliamentary immunity as soon as he landed in Santiago. Judge Guzman Tapia told reporters that illness was not cause for dismissal of charges under Chilean law.

By February, the Pinochet case had taken one more unexpected turn. Vigorous legal appeals by the Belgian government which, along with Spain, wanted to extradite Pinochet for trial, prevailed in blocking the dictator's hasty return to Santiago. The medical report kept secret by the British government was made accessible to the courts of the other European governments seeking a trial for Pinochet and it quickly leaked. While the report indicated that Pinochet had suffered some brain damage in his deteriorated condition, it also became a subject of complicated legal and medical dispute. In the end, the British government decided to wash its hands of the dictator, and in early March Straw released Pinochet from custody and returned him to Chile, a free man

Pinochet's plane approached Santiago just days before the presidential inauguration of Ricardo Lagos. Defying a plea from Lagos' transition team to keep Pinochet's arrival a low-key event, the top commanders of Chile's armed forces traveled, along with a military brass band, to personally welcome the dictator back home. Once again, Pinochet was greeted to the tune of his favorite "Lilli Marlene." The cameras snapped and whirred as Pinochet's wheelchair descended onto the tarmac. And then, as if experiencing a miraculous recovery from his supposedly debilitating illness, Pinochet arose from his wheelchair, briskly crossed the runway, and heartily and personally greeted every one of his assembled well-wishers. Newspapers around the world flashed pictures of the General's unrepentant act of arrogance in not having even the minimum discretion to play along with the story of his being too weak to stand trial.

The incoming Lagos administration freely vented its rage at both Pinochet and the military command for having staged their televised airport show. Human rights groups vowed to step up the pressure on the General.

And, indeed, General Pinochet's triumph in winning his release from Britain expressed by the little victory jig he performed at the airport was short-lived. His 503 days of detention in Britain had completely eroded his power, his position, his legend. The artifice of impunity and unaccountability that he had carefully constructed over twenty years was dealt a shattering blow by his arrest, had begun to crumble during his stay in custody, and was now well on its way, irretrievably, to its end.

Within days of Pinochet's return, the newly invigorated Chilean judicial system began to call him to account. The unthinkable was now happening. Judge Juan Guzman Tapia, who was coordinating the scores of criminal complaints lodged against Pinochet, immediately filed briefs to strip the self-appointed Senator for Life of his parliamentary immunity – the first prerequisite to putting him on trial. As the Santiago Appeals Court deliberated the matter, Chile held its breath. And case after case began to pile up against Pinochet, more than a hundred within a few weeks.

Meanwhile, the network of terror engineered by Pinochet continued to unravel. On May 11, former military junta member and director of Pinochet's CNI secret police, retired

General Humberto Gordon, was indicted for the 1986 murder of four Chilean leftists. (He died, discredited, only weeks later.)

Thousands of formerly classified documents being released by the US government revealed ever more details about the inner workings of Operation Condor – the continent-wide murder consortium set up by Chile and neighboring dictatorships in the 1970s.

Argentine judge Maria Servini de Cubria broke new ground in clarifying the Pinochet regime's direct involvement in the 1974 assassination of former Chilean General Carlos Prats. And forty-eight documents obtained by Servini, including a memo directly implicating Pinochet in the 1976 Washington DC car-bomb murder of Orlando Letelier, were handed over to US investigators.

Even more ominous for Pinochet and his surviving closest collaborators, around the time of the General's return to Chile, the US Justice Department dispatched two assistant US attorneys and three FBI agents to Santiago to interrogate forty-two people, many of them former military officers, thought to have information about or participation in the Letelier murder.

Then, in May of 2000, came the bombshell news. The Santiago Appeals Court had ruled to strip Pinochet of his parliamentary immunity, thereby exposing him directly to trial. In August the Chilean Supreme Court, once a docile tool of the dictatorship, upheld the verdict against Pinochet by a 14–6 vote. By September, arrangements were being made to submit the former General to a series of mental tests that were prerequisite to eventual trial. By then, the number of cases pending against him had swollen to 164.

Pinochet might still be found too feeble to go into the dock. But as Viviana Diaz, leader of the Association of Relatives of the Disappeared, jubilantly put it: "It looks like General Pinochet will spend the rest of his life fighting every day, every hour, to avoid that trial." Upon hearing of the Supreme Court ruling against the former dictator, Isabel Allende, the daughter of former President Salvador Allende, said "This day marks the end of impunity."

But perhaps the most dramatic sign that General Pinochet had definitively lost the battle for his political legacy came from Washington. His most ardent historical defender, his most loyal and powerful ally, the US government, had formally joined the list of his potential persecutors. During Pinochet's detention in London, the US government had been conspicuously absent from the list of countries demanding his extradition. At one point, the Clinton administration made a plea for mercy, asking that, for humanitarian reasons, the General be sent home to Chile. But all this time, a small group of Justice Department investigators remained determined to press long-standing accusations against the former Chilean dictator. After all, by any available and logical evidence, Pinochet had master-minded the *only* act of international terrorism carried out in the US capital – the 1976 carbomb murder of Orlando Letelier. Apparently, those determined Justice Department officials carried the day. On May 28 2000, the *Washington Post* reported that:

> Federal investigators have uncovered evidence that some of
> them believe is sufficient to indict Gen. Augusto Pinochet

for conspiracy to commit murder in the 1976 car bombing that killed . . . Orlando Letelier, on Washington's Embassy Row . . . Justice Department officials said they do not minimize the difficulty of indicting Pinochet for acts that took place 24 years ago in a foreign country. And even if he is indicted, the officials said, a trail in the United States is highly unlikely because he recently was excused from trial in Britain on grounds of ill health and has returned to Chile . . . Still, the officials said, Attorney General Janet Reno is committed to pursuing the investigation of the Letelier assassination, which the Justice Department considers a state-sponsored act of terrorism on U.S. soil . . .

Regardless of whether the US legally indicts Pinochet, in late September of 2000 the CIA released a report that morally excoriated not only the dictator's regime but the American spy agency itself. Under the terms of a measure sponsored by New York Congressman Maurice Hinchey, the American spy agency for the first time in twenty-seven years was forced to openly reveal crucial details of its cozy relationship with the Chilean military dictatorship.

The new report, "CIA Activities in Chile," finally confirmed what we have all assumed but could never prove. "CIA actively supported the military Junta after the overthrow of Allende," said the report. "Many of Pinochet's officers were involved in systematic and widespread human rights abuses . . . Some of these were contacts or agents of the CIA or US military."

The most damaging news in the report was that the head of Chile's secret police, General Manuel Contreras, was not only a paid CIA asset at the time his own agents carried out the Letelier car-bombing in Washington but that the agency's contact with him continued long after the bloody assassination.

The report also formally confirmed for the first time that the CIA was, in fact, "aware" of the plotting that led to the 1973 coup; that within a year after the coup the CIA knew of Chile's efforts to construct the continent-wide network of secret terror known as Operation Condor; that the CIA had provided a payment of $35,000 in "humanitarian aid" to a group of coup plotters in 1970 after that same group had already assassinated then Army Commander René Schneider; that the CIA was involved in a campaign to influence Chilean media against Allende; and that the CIA had knowledge of the wholesale murder being carried out in the first days of the dictatorship by Pinochet confidant General Arellano Stark (a revelation sure to be used in the ongoing prosecution of the same former General). As this book goes to press, yet another "document dump" from formerly secret US government files on Chile is about to take place and, no matter how partial, it can only serve to fill in more of the historical blanks left gaping for the last thirty years.

Two years ago, when General Pinochet was being clapped into British custody, it was clear that everything we had come to think and know about Chile was about to radically change. But just how it would play out was unknown. And yet, in even the most optimistic scenarios spun out at the time (and Heaven knows that those of us intimately tied to Chile were feverish in our conjecture), we could not at that time even remotely imagine just what momentous consequences this arrest would eventually unleash. I would not have dared to imagine that it would eventually become the catalyst to what now seems a recovery of Chile's collective consciousness and dignity. Even less did I hazard to think that detaining the old dictator in the London Clinic that evening would set off a chain of events that would shed so much light on one of the darkest chapters of American Cold War foreign policy.

And yet, it has. Peter Kornbluh, the Chile expert at the non-profit National Security Archive who has lobbied for full declassification of Chile documents, said that the new CIA report makes the clearest case to date that the agency, under orders from the Nixon administration, played an important role in supporting the Pinochet dictatorship. "This report is the genie out of the bottle," he said, "and it can't be put back in."

In the foothills of the towering Andes, on a windswept rise on the extreme eastern boundary of Santiago, sit the remains of Villa Grimaldi. I've wanted to come here before but could never summon the fortitude to visit what was one of the primary tor-ture centres of Pinochet's regime. I had personally known too many people who had passed through this maze of terror or others similar to it that scarred the map of Chile in the Seventies and Eighties.

A bright yellow fence now encloses the grounds which have been renamed by human rights groups as the Park of Memory.

It's mostly a sandy plaza with the stumps of the old Villa's foundations puncturing the earth. The dark, mammoth mansion that sprawled over the bulk of the lot was razed after Pinochet's fall.

The new life here – some scrawny striplings and some rose bushes – seems as tenuous as civic life itself in the Chile outside the fence. A plaque at the entrance, placed by the human rights activists who set up the park, reads: "This place where today stands a park was, a few years ago, a place of torture and cruelty. It honours the dead, as well as the anguished memory of some survivors of the former Villa Grimaldi. Each flower watered with the tears of yesterday is firm commitment that here, never, never again!"

A narrow circular path leads the visitor on what can only be called a tour of barbarity. The plaques along the way are numbing: "Place of torture and hangings" . . . "The tower: place of solitary torture and extermination" . . . "Place of hangings" . . . "Torture chamber" . . . "Annex torture chamber" . . . "Women's cells 1 × 1 meter" . . . "The Grill: electrical beds."

At the end of the path, a wall. Engraved on the wall the names of the more than 200 Chileans "disappeared or executed who passed through Villa Grimaldi 1974–1978." In alphabetical order from René Roberto Acuña to Mario Luis Quezada. I am tempted to scan the rest of the list for familiar names of long-lost friends and colleagues but I decide to let that thought go.

The wall, the park in its entirety, is a quiet but deeply moving monument to Chile's martyrs. But it's also safely segregated, tucked away on this distant suburban hilltop. The park receives little foot traffic. And some days it is simply pad-locked.

Chile is a country that was ripped apart from within. The pain was so great, the horrors so chilling, the brutality and hypocrisy so shocking that it is hard to comprehend, even today, twenty-five years after the worst excesses. The establishment of living monuments like this park is only a first and incomplete step toward healing. No organism, not the human body nor the body politic of a nation, is every really healed until the illness is identified, isolated, and expunged. Chile will be whole not when more visitors show up to Villa Grimaldi on their weekends off. Nor when school children are bussed in for a quick walking tour. No. Chile will only be whole when the fence around Villa Grimaldi is finally torn down and the horrifying truths and consequences contained within are fully exposed to the society around it.

The struggle for Chile's future resides in interpreting its past. As the inscription on the wall of the disappeared cautions: "The forgotten past is full of memory."

ACKNOWLEDGMENTS

There simply isn't enough room here to list all those who, over a span of thirty years, helped in some way or another to make this book possible. But there are some to whom I want to extend special gratitude.

During the Allende period in Chile I was well taken care of and looked after by Juan Ibañez and Mario Dujisin of the Oficina de Información y Radiodifusión de la Presidencia de la República. My eternal gratitude for the trust and confidence they invested in a twenty-one-year-old gringo. Thanks also to Jorge Uribe from the same office and with whom, a decade after the coup, I was able to survive some scintillating moments in the hilly underbrush of El Salvador. My initially parochial perspectives were widened by association with my Argentine comrades and Santiago room-mates Susana and Carlos "Django" Luna. Orlando Jofre opened many doors and took me boldly across the economic and sociological borders of Chile's apartheid-like divides. Thanks also to my friends in the Santiago Centro section of the Socialist Party, who gave me a priceless

ACKNOWLEDGMENTS

political education. Patricia Vargas made the last two agonizing months of the Allende period (and the ensuing twenty-seven years) all very liveable.

A lot of Americans my age – and not always my age – floated through Chile in the days of Allende. I had little contact with most of them. But a handful offered insights and friendships I have cherished. Among them: Vince Santilli, Leslie Krebs, Paul Heath Hoeffell, and John Dinges. A million thanks to Melvin Blum, wherever you are, for many unforgettable days and nights, especially those spent hiding in your house eating onions and drinking Pisco during the first days of Pinochet. Dennis Allred, eternal gratitude for the protection and refuge you offered me. Thank you for literally saving my life. Thanks to my friends in the Mexican diplomatic service who got me out of Chile.

During the post-Allende period, the best insight, the best hospitality and the best of friendships has always been offered by Tim Frasca. Thanks also to "la vieja Elena" who is a constant reminder of everything that is wonderful about wonderful people. Jonathan Franklin provided great ground assistance and even better analysis. Thanks also to Irene Geiss, Carmen Soria, Hector Salazar, and Ricardo Israel.

The shared insights and work of Saul Landau, Peter Kornbluh, and Ariel Dorfman are always illuminating and inspiring.

During the long, dark years of dictatorship and exile Robert Naduris and Juan "Comandante" Rojas, against all odds, kept us all together in body, mind, and spirit. Roberto, be assured that your fine children carry on your legacy. Thanks also to Suzi

Weissman, who can always find the most optimistic explanation for almost anything.

Over the years my work on Chile has been supported by numerous magazine editors. Thanks to Jonathan Z. Larsen and Dan Bischoff, with whom I worked at the *Village Voice*, to Tom Frank and "Diamonds" Mulcahey at *The Baffler*, and Roger Cohn and Jonathan King at *Mother Jones*.

Very special thanks to my current overseers at *The Nation* magazine, Victor Navasky and Katrina vanden Heuvel. They have been more than generous and supportive of my work on Chile and just about everything else. It is a privilege to work for and with them.

Thanks to Colin Robinson at Verso for thinking up this book. Gavin Browning did a magician's work conjuring up some of this material from obscure archives.

And finally, a special nod of gratitude to the former Governor of the State of California, Ronald Reagan. Thanks to his direct intervention in the spring of 1971, and by his executive order, I was pitched out of the California State University system for my anti-war activities. As a result of that expulsion, I discovered Chile.

Gipper, this one's for you.

Printed in the United States
by Baker & Taylor Publisher Services